(a word to describe me)
(my name)
AF585129

My progress chart

Find the letter to match your completed page. Track the letter and colour the picture.

a b c d

p o n m

q r s t

2

e f g h
i j k l
u v w
x y z

Help each animal find its home.

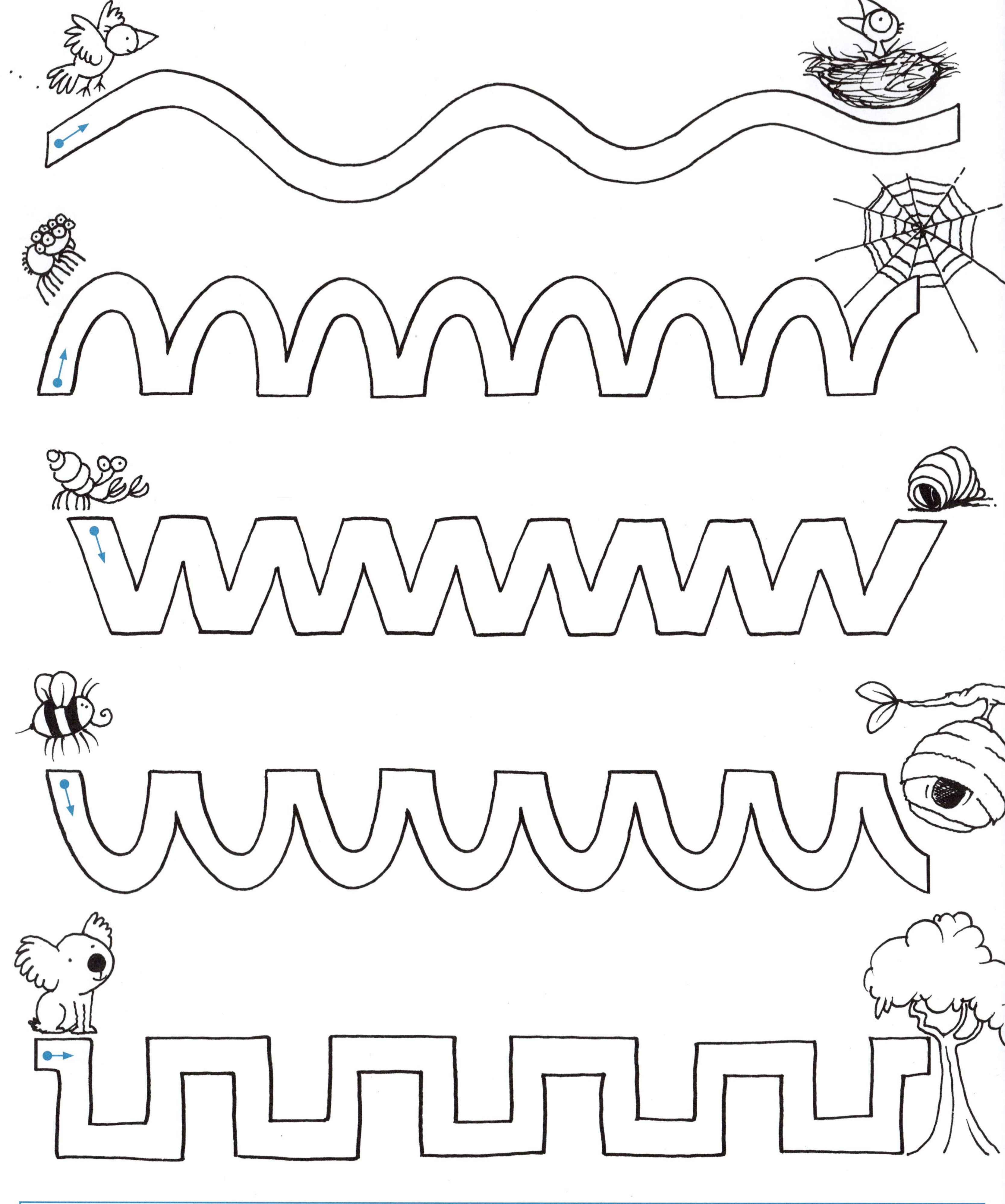

Handwriting: Tracking; left to right direction; fine motor control.

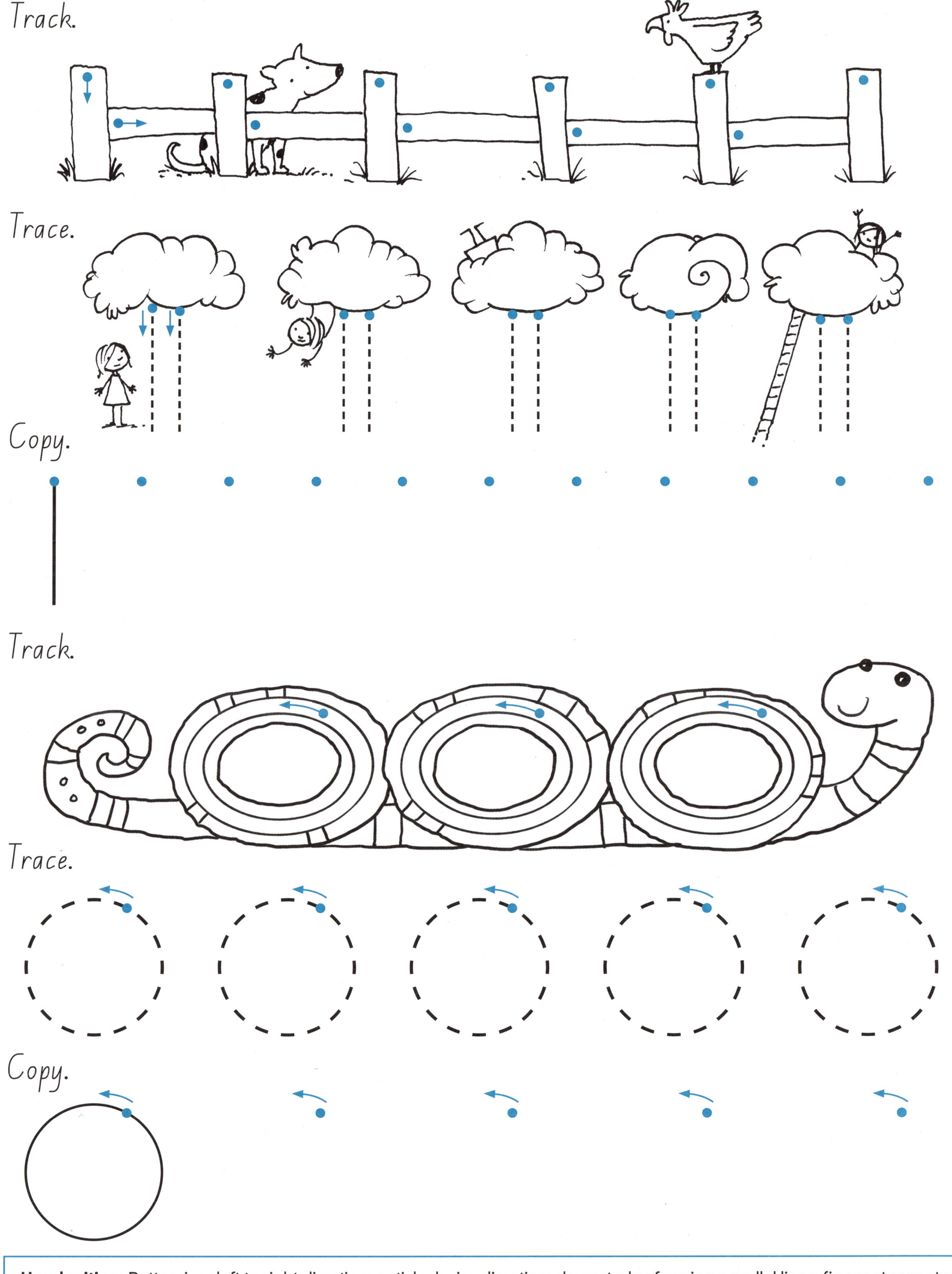

Handwriting: Patterning; left to right direction; anticlockwise direction; downstroke; forming parallel lines; fine motor control.

Trace.

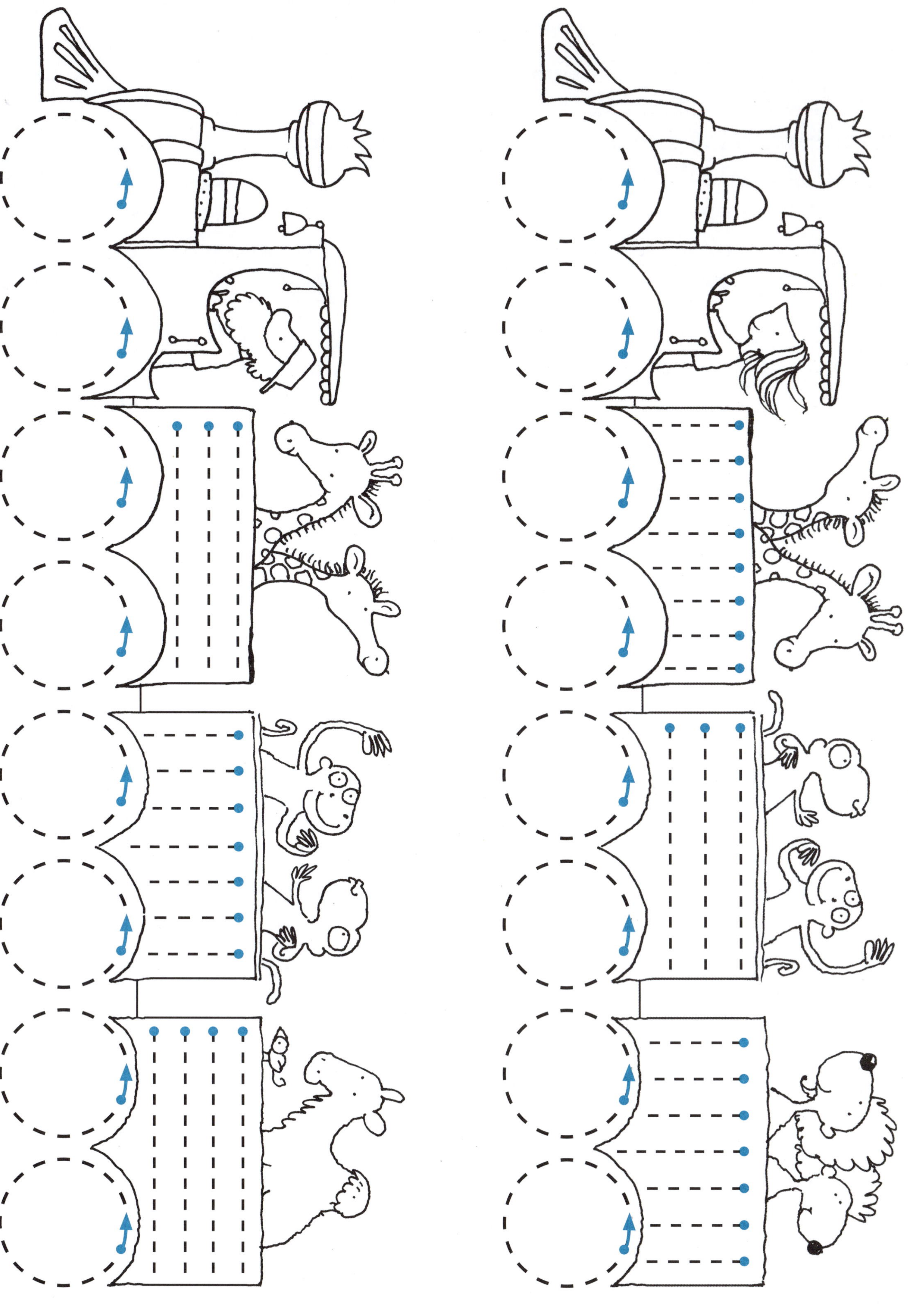

Handwriting: Patterning; downstroke and anticlockwise movements; left to right direction; forming parallel lines; fine motor control.

Trace.

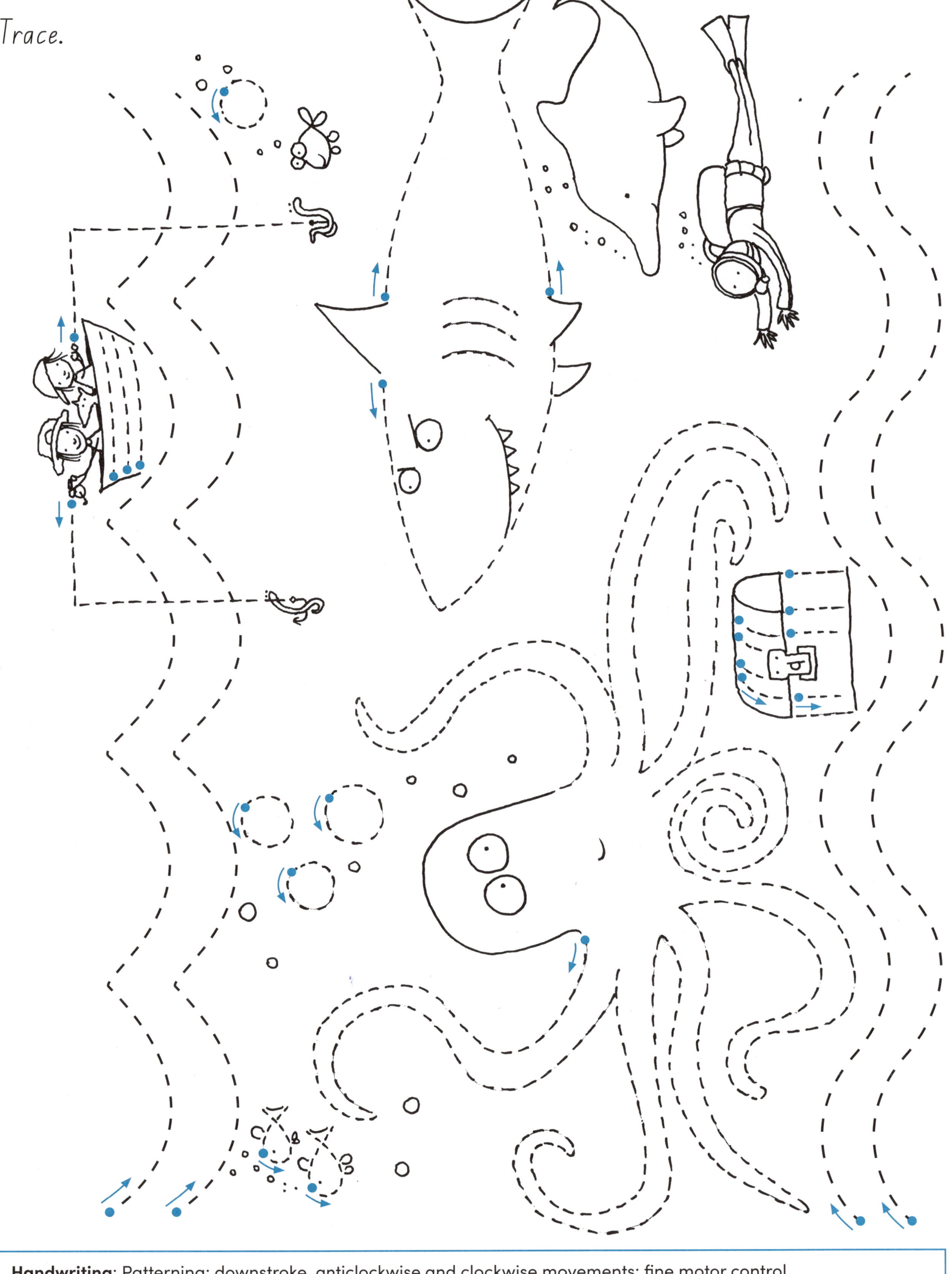

Handwriting: Patterning; downstroke, anticlockwise and clockwise movements; fine motor control.

Phonic chant

messy monkey
m m m

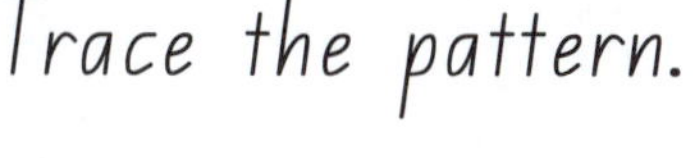

Trace the pattern.

Trace the pattern. Keep your pencil on the page.

Trace the pattern. Turn each pattern into a picture.

Track.

Handwriting: clockwise letter; body letter (m).
Vocabulary on page: messy, monkey.
Extra vocabulary: mat, mop, man, am, mum, men, him, many, munch.

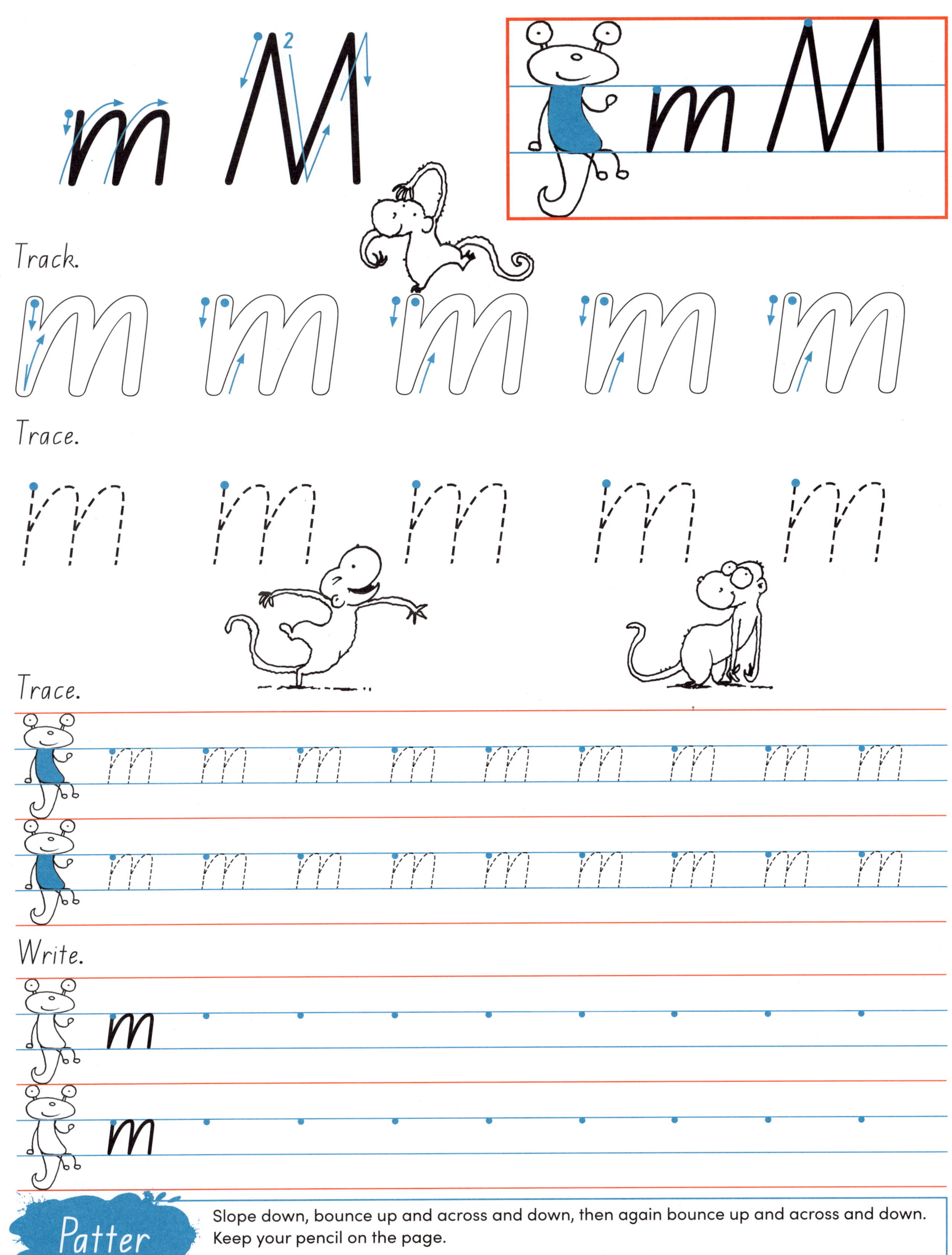

Patter

Slope down, bounce up and across and down, then again bounce up and across and down. Keep your pencil on the page.

Phonic chant

noisy numbat
n n n

Track the pattern.

Trace the pattern. Keep your pencil on the page.

Copy the pattern. Turn each pattern into a picture.

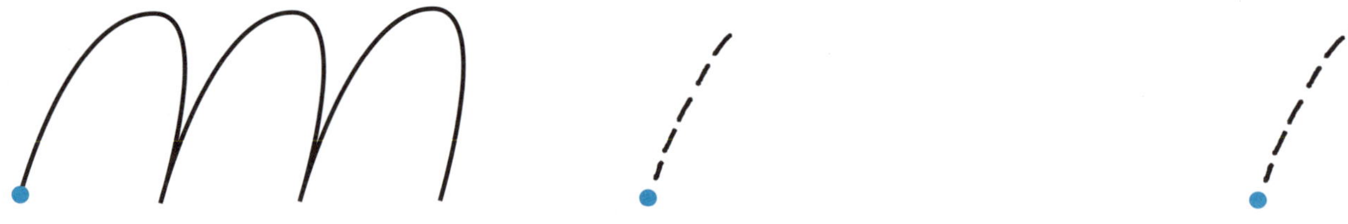

Track.

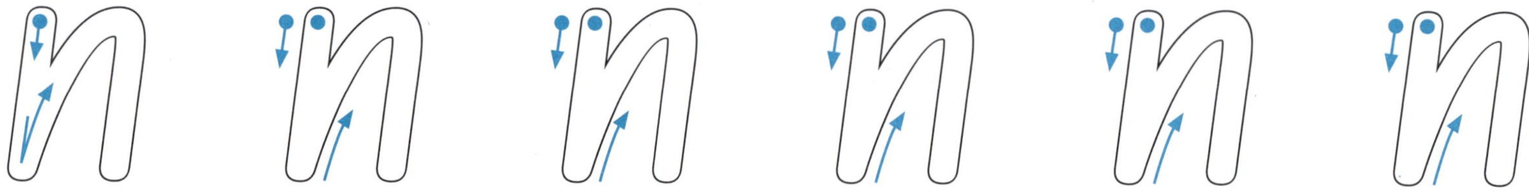

Handwriting: clockwise letter; body letter (n).
Vocabulary: noisy, numbat. The word *numbat* is based on the word *noombat* from the Noongar language.
Phonic knowledge /n/: no, not, nip, nap, nod, an, can, pan, in, pin, tin, sun, run.

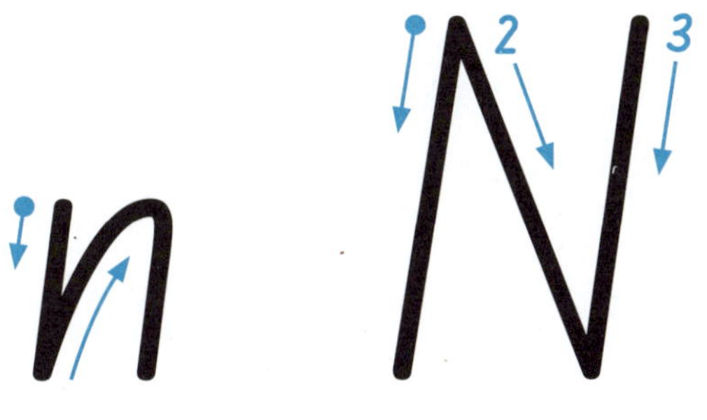

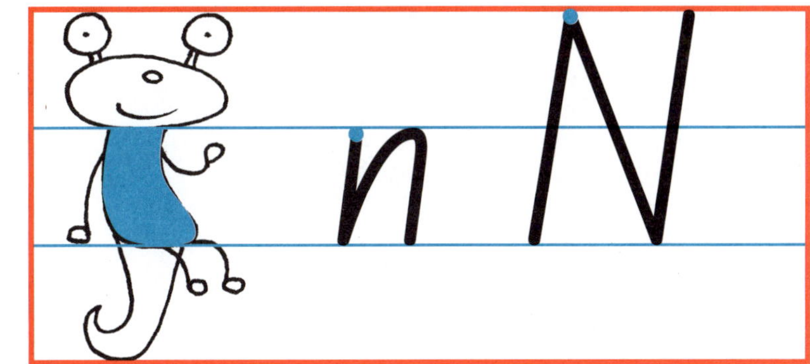

Track.

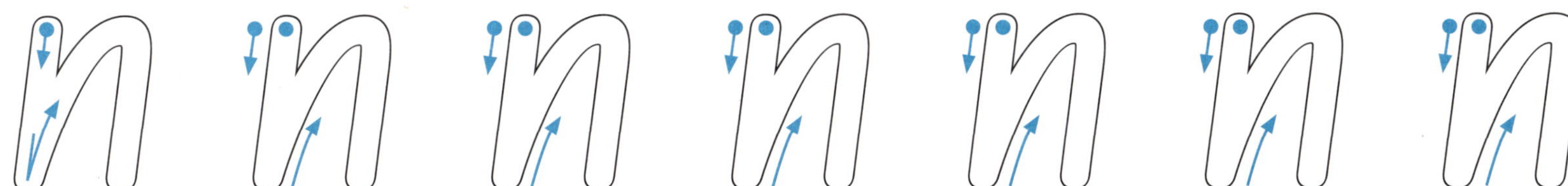

Trace.

Trace.

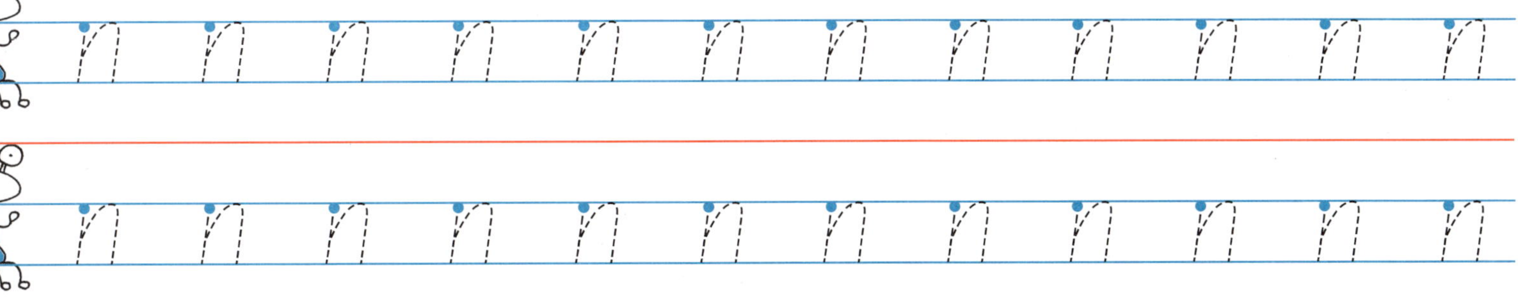

Write.

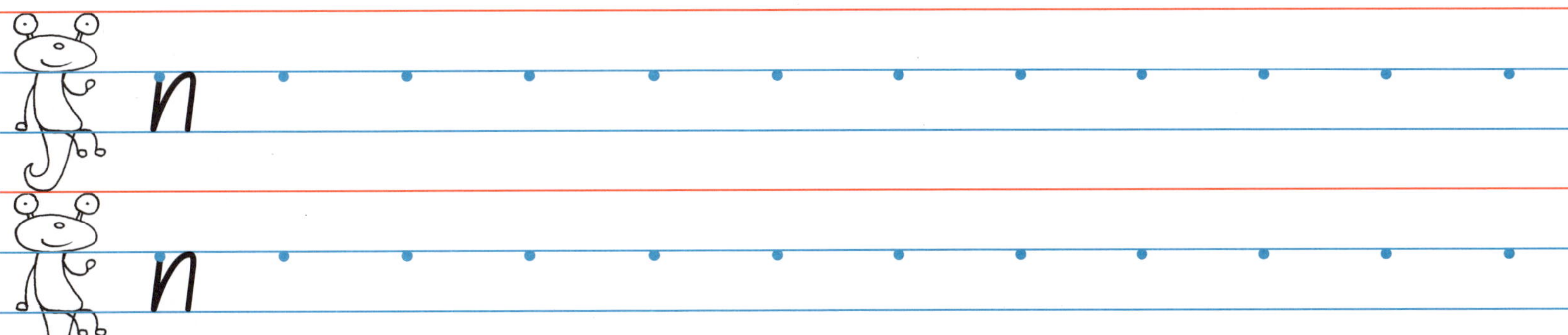

Patter

Slope down, then go up and across the top and down again. Keep your pencil on the page.

Phonic chant

hairy hen

h h h

Trace the pattern.

Trace the pattern. Keep your pencil on the page.

Trace then copy the pattern.

Track.

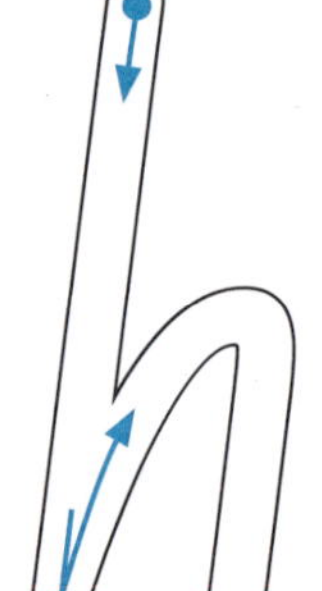    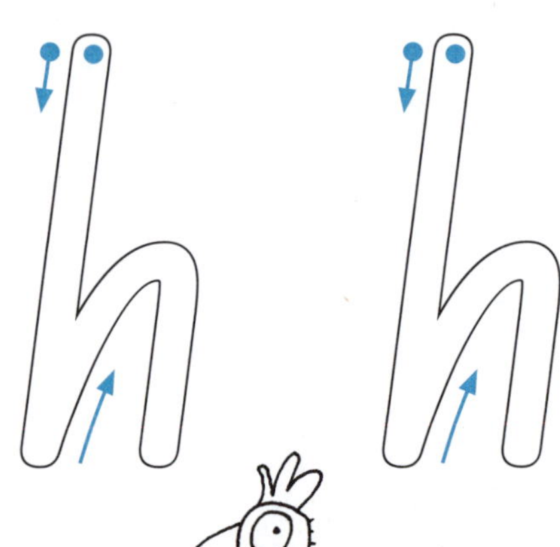

Handwriting: clockwise letter; head and body letter (ascender) (h).
Vocabulary: hay, hairy, have, help.
Phonic knowledge /h/: hen, hop, hat, hot, hit, hug, hum, he, him, has, had.

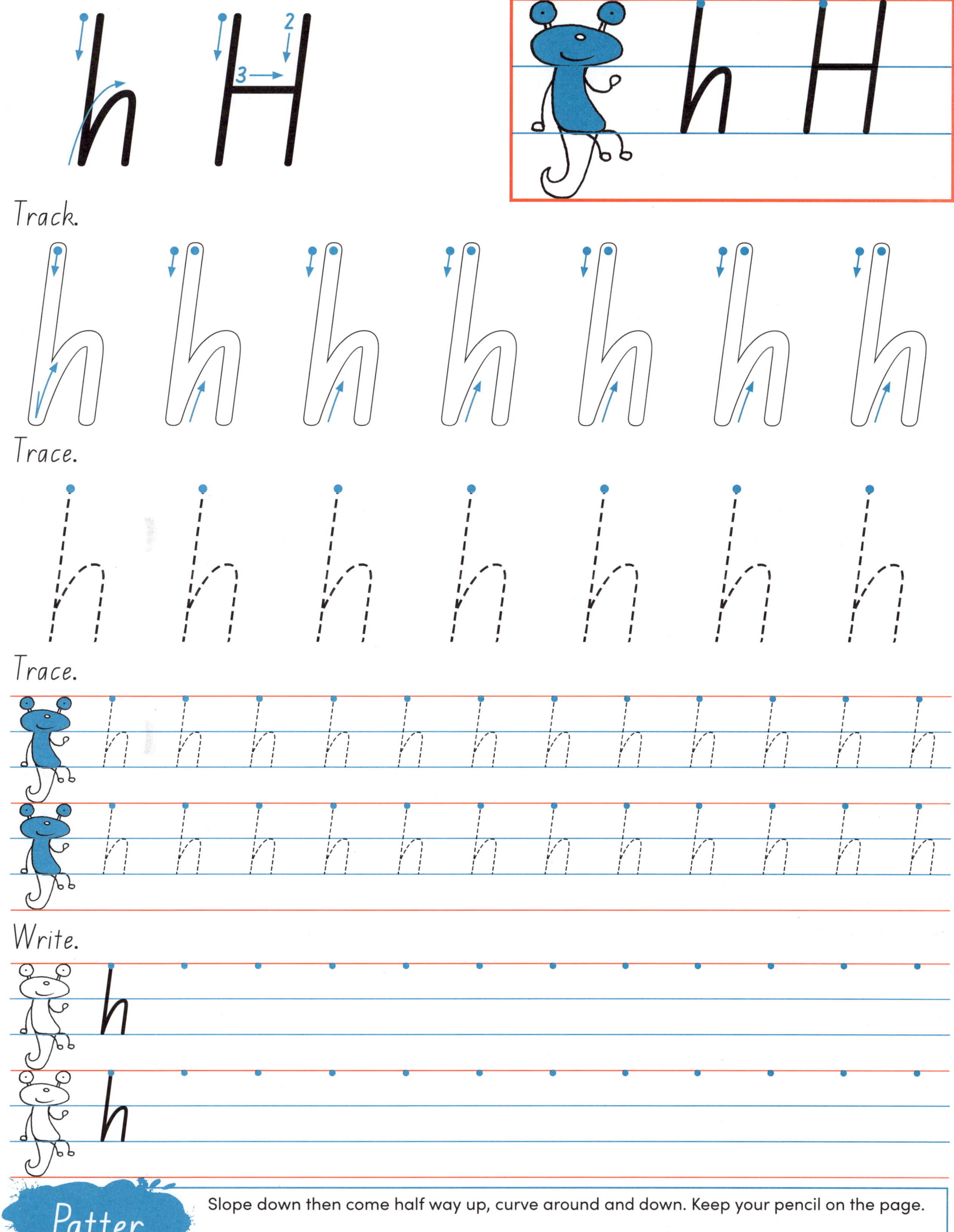

Slope down then come half way up, curve around and down. Keep your pencil on the page.

Phonic chant

kind koala

k k k

Trace the pattern. Finish the kites.

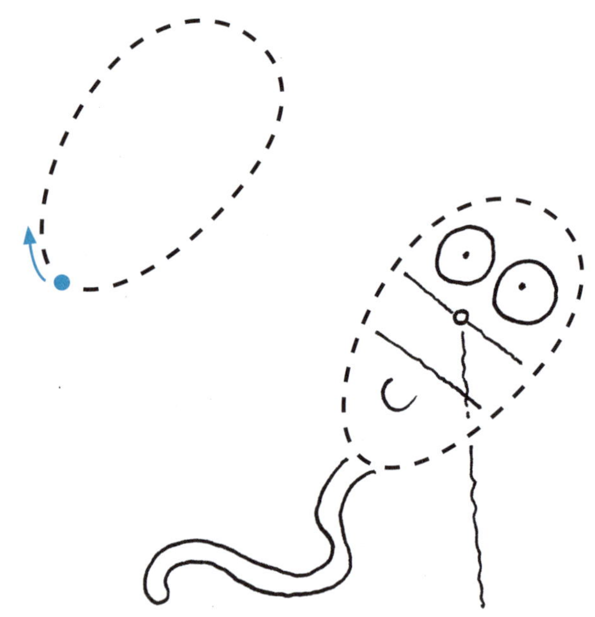

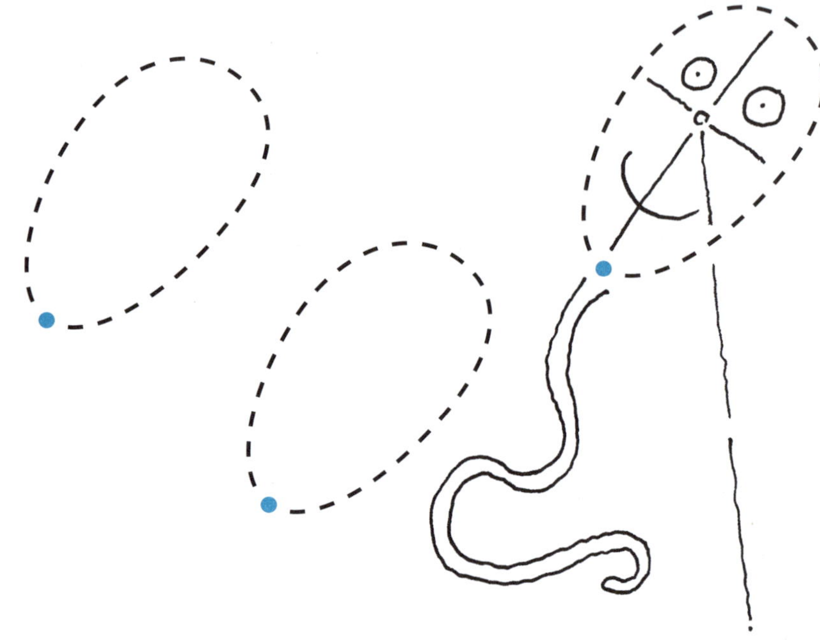

Trace the pattern.

Track.

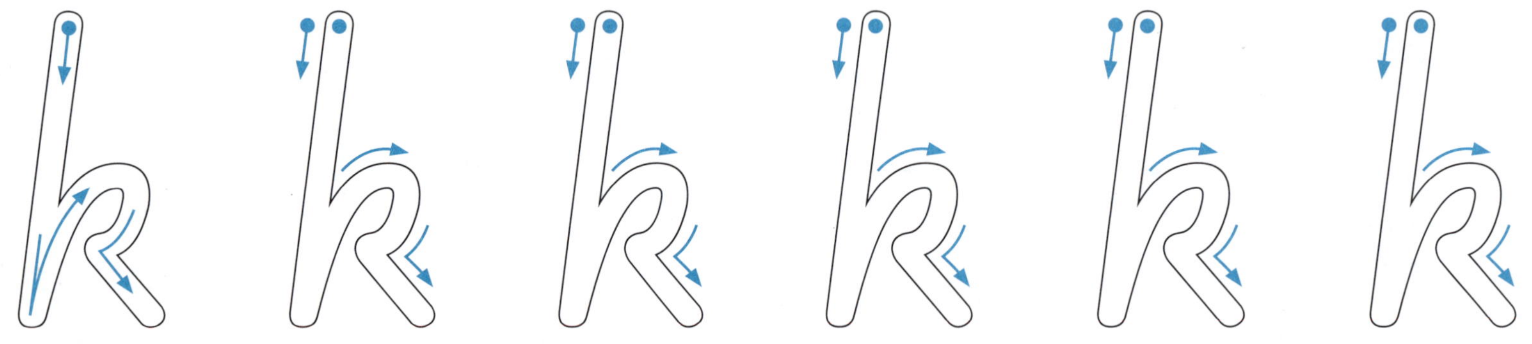

Handwriting: clockwise letter; head and body letter (ascender) (k). **Vocabulary:** kind, koala, kangaroo, kite, key, kitten. The word *koala* is based on the word *gula* from the Dharug language. Gula means 'no water'.
Phonic knowledge /k/: kit, king, kid.

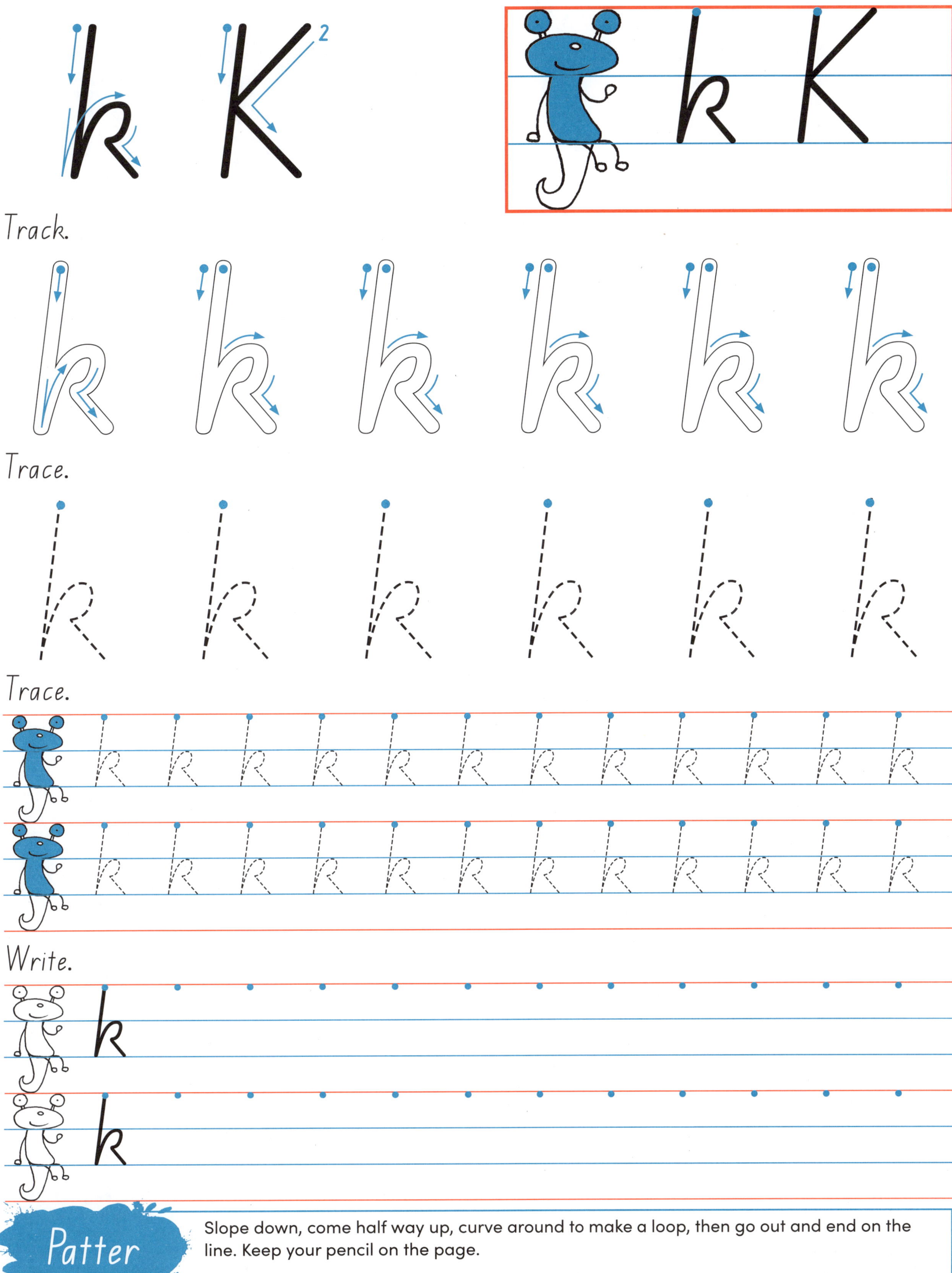

Patter

Slope down, come half way up, curve around to make a loop, then go out and end on the line. Keep your pencil on the page.

Phonic chant

pretty pig
p p p

Trace the pattern. Keep your pencil on the page.

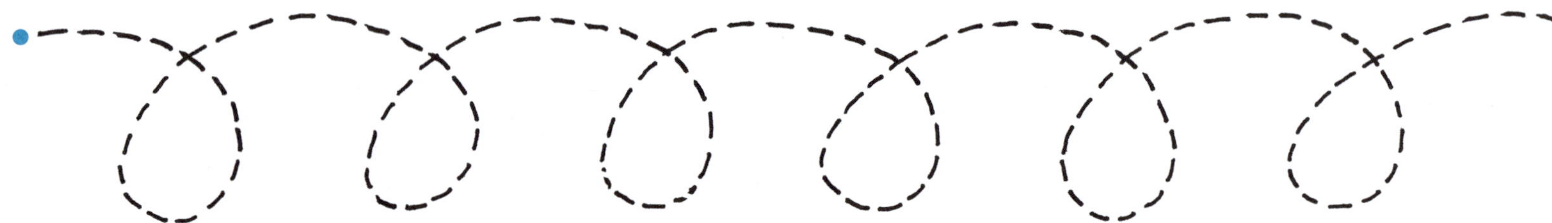

Trace the patterns.

Copy the pattern.

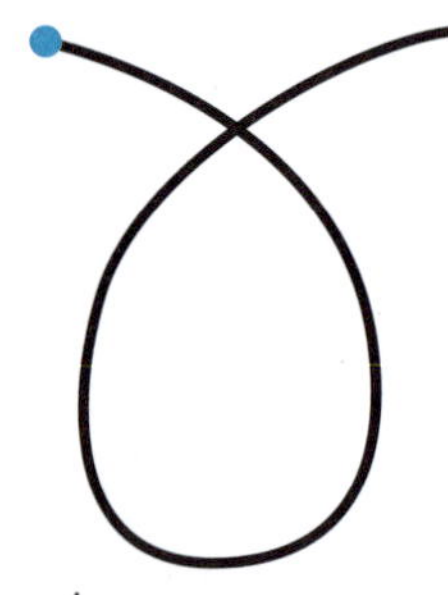

Track.

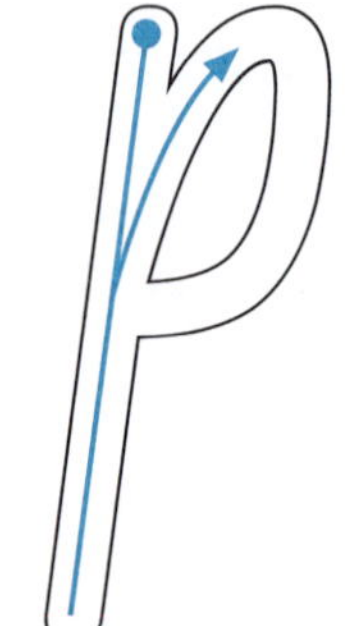
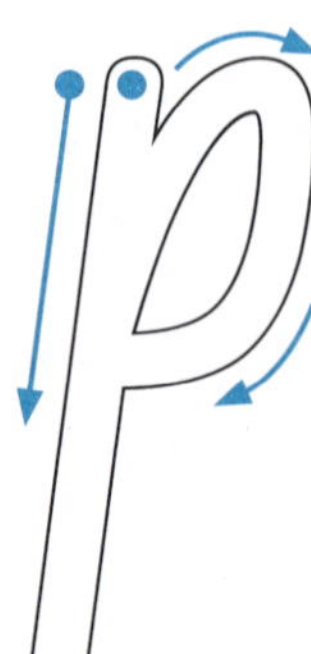
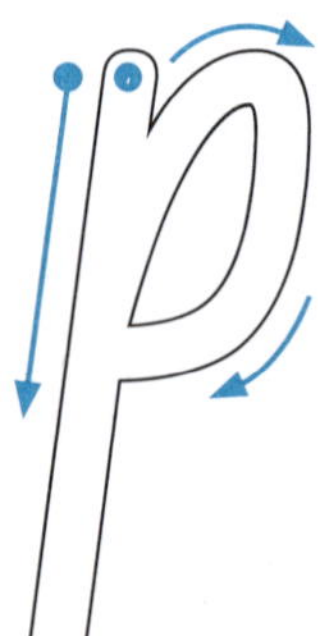

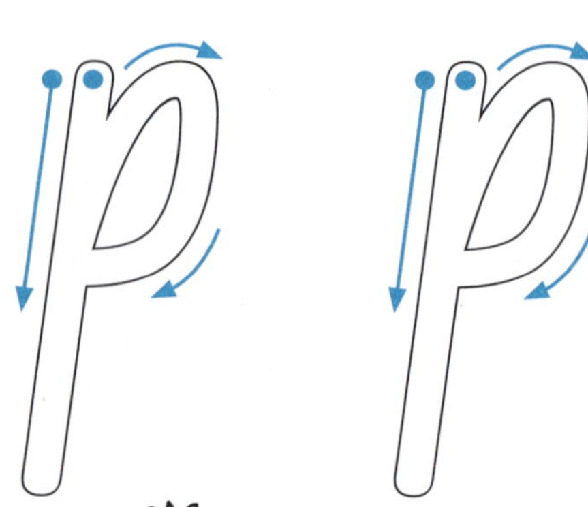

Handwriting: clockwise letter; body and tail letter (descender) (p).
Vocabulary: pretty, pink, prickly.
Phonic knowledge /p/: pig, pat, pit, pot, put, pan, pop, map, nip, top, tap.

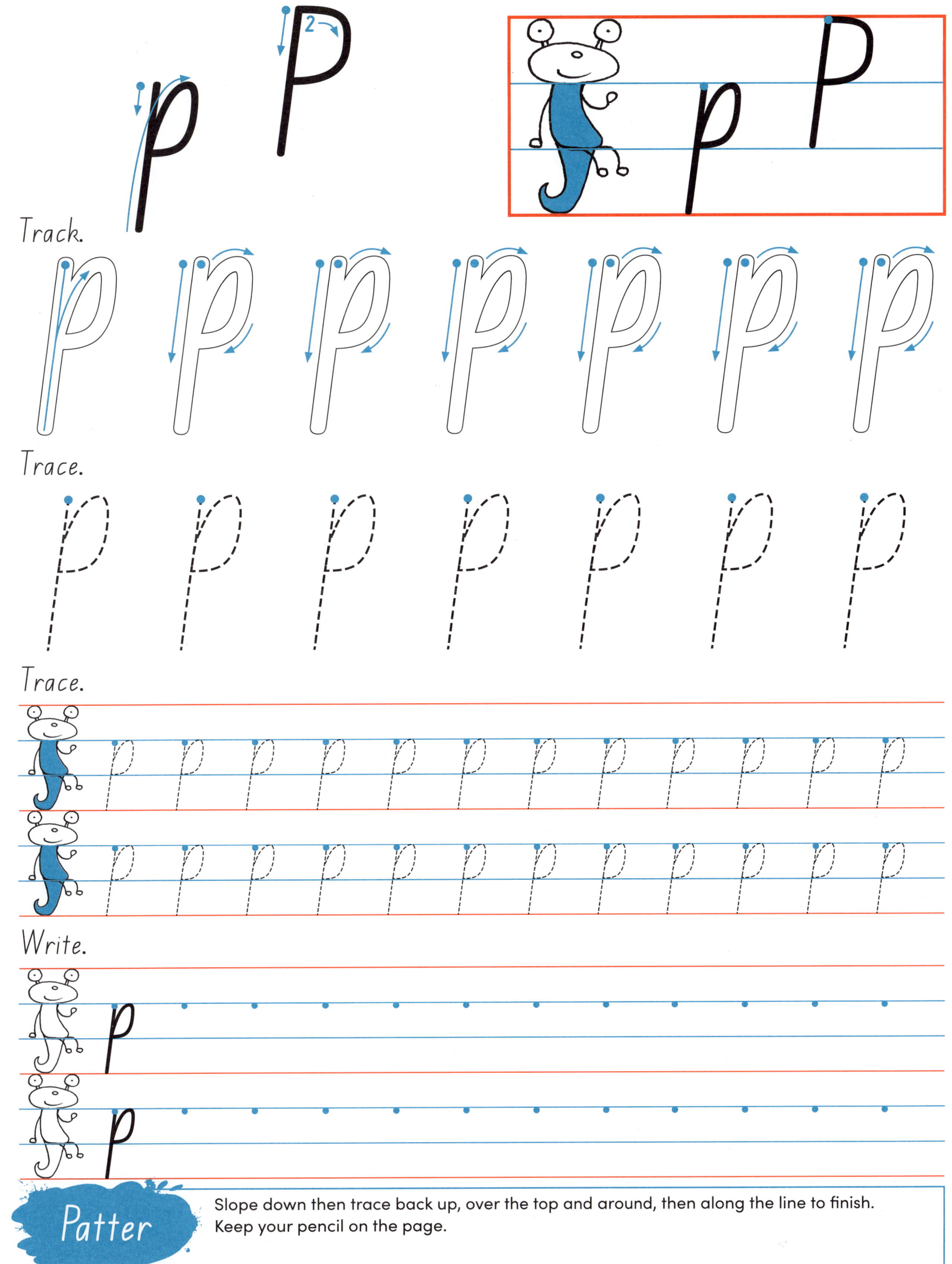

Patter

Slope down then trace back up, over the top and around, then along the line to finish. Keep your pencil on the page.

Phonic chant

bouncy bear
b b b

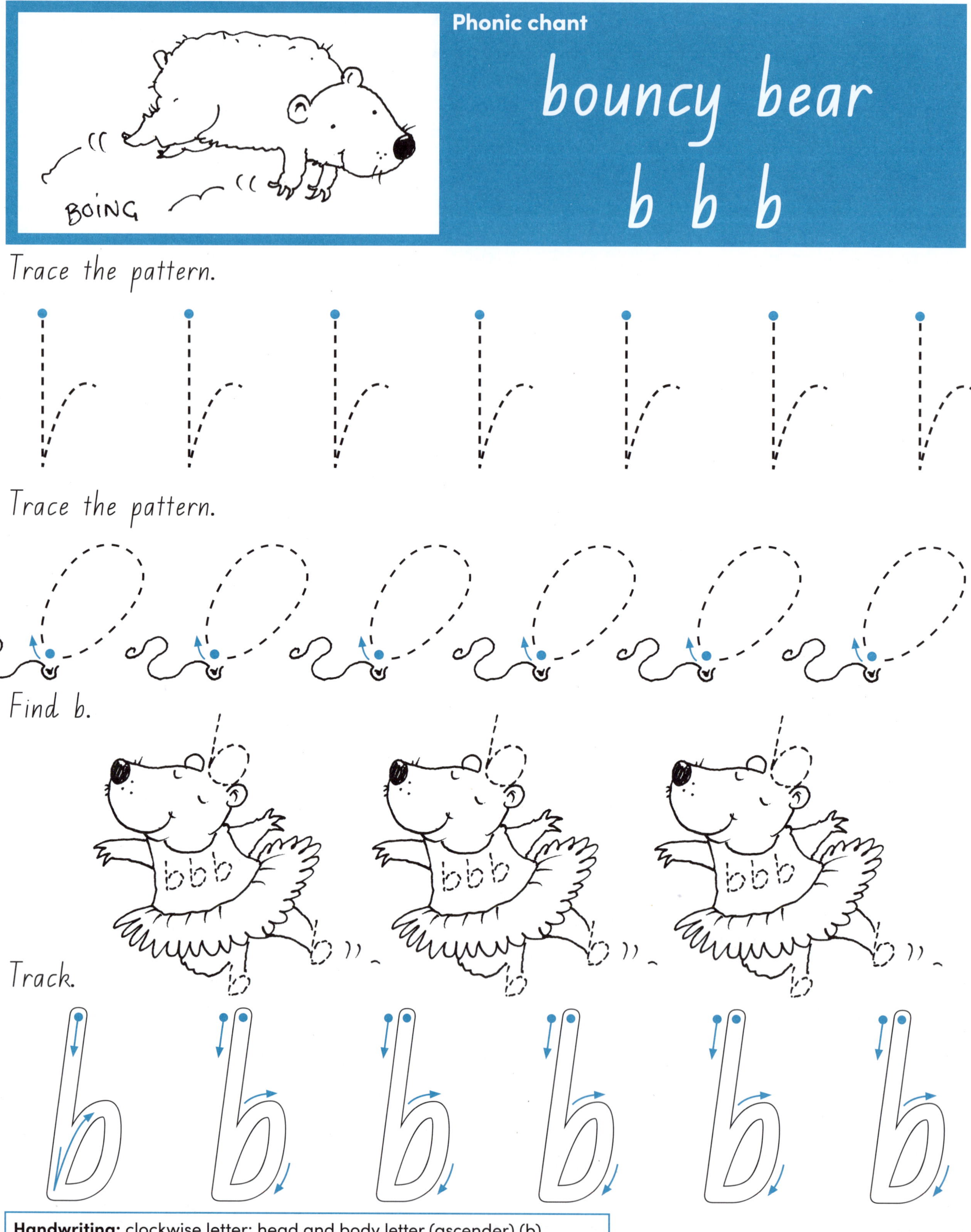

Trace the pattern.

Trace the pattern.

Find b.

Track.

Handwriting: clockwise letter; head and body letter (ascender) (b).
Vocabulary: bear, balloon, ballet, bouncy, bobcat, back.
Phonic knowledge /b/: be, bee, by, bat, big, bed, but, bug , bag, bad, bus.

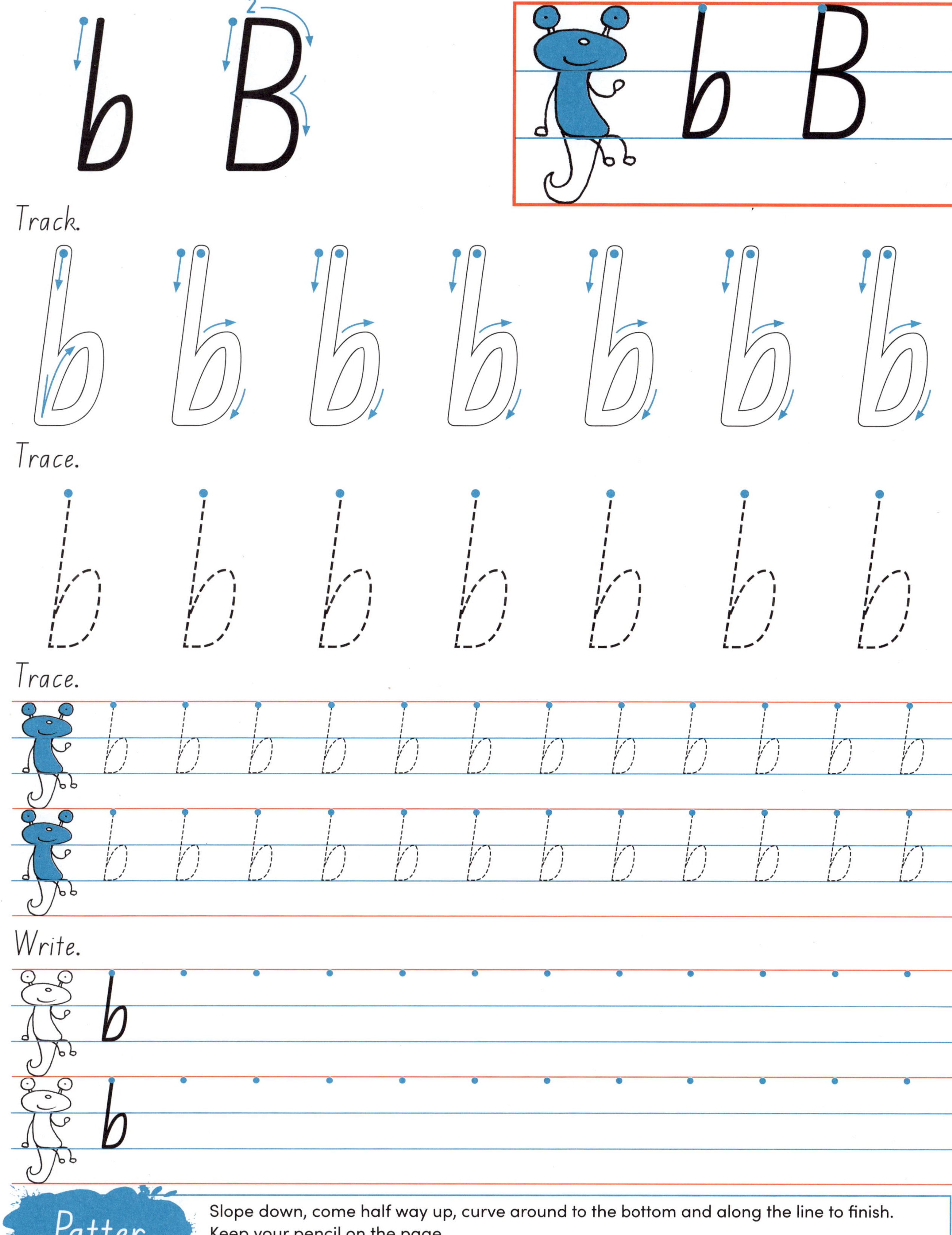

Patter

Slope down, come half way up, curve around to the bottom and along the line to finish. Keep your pencil on the page.

Phonic chant

rapid rat
r r r

Trace the pattern.

Find r.

Track.

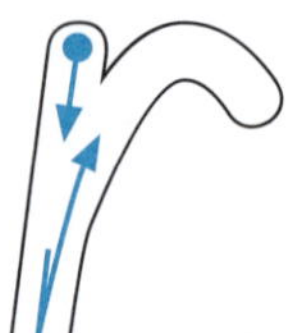 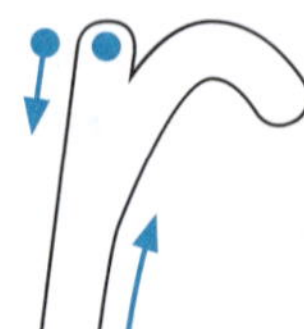 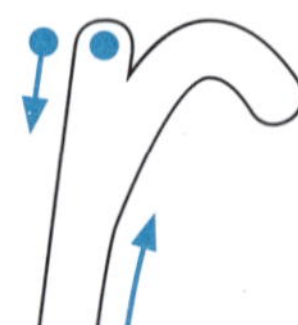 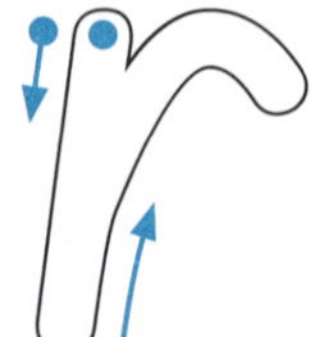 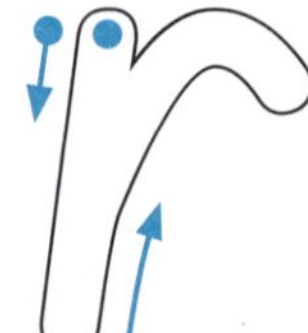 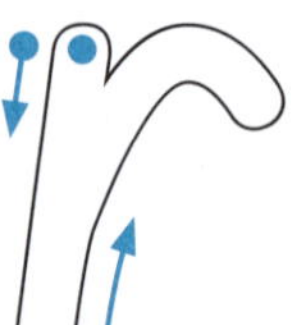

Handwriting: clockwise letter; body letter (r).
Vocabulary: race, rapid, raft.
Phonic knowledge /r/: red, rat, rip, run, ran, ram, rug, rot, drip, drop.

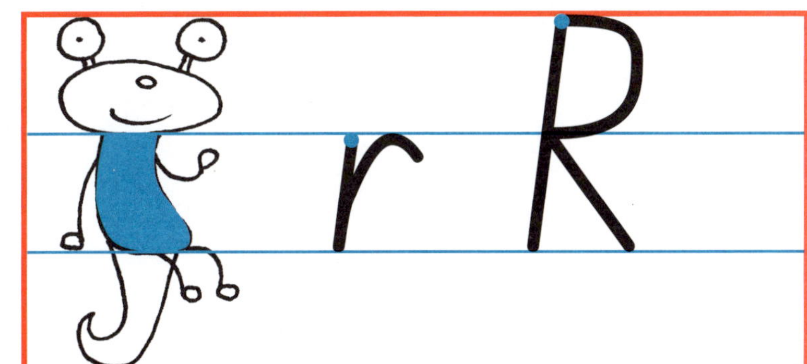

Track.

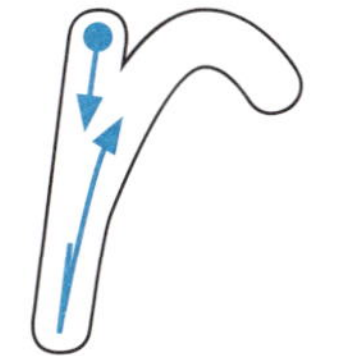  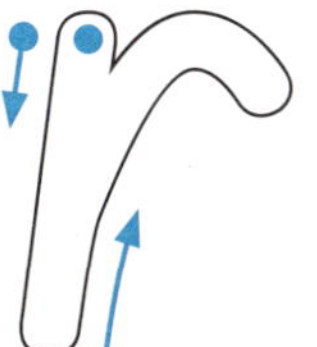 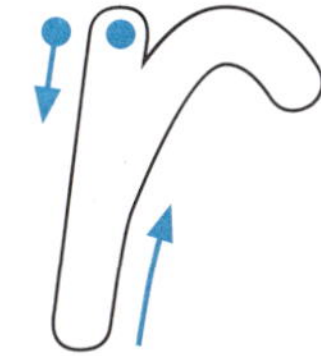 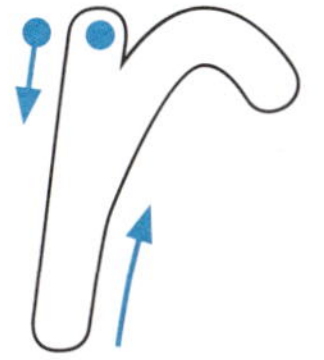 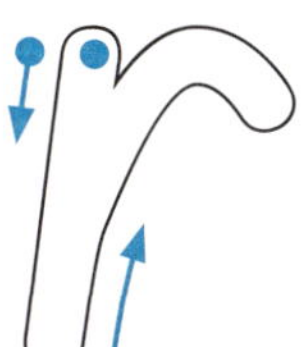 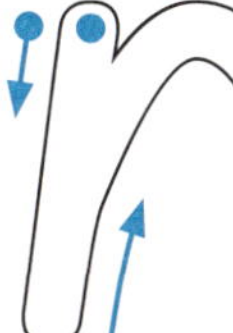

Trace.

 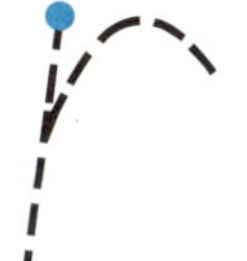      

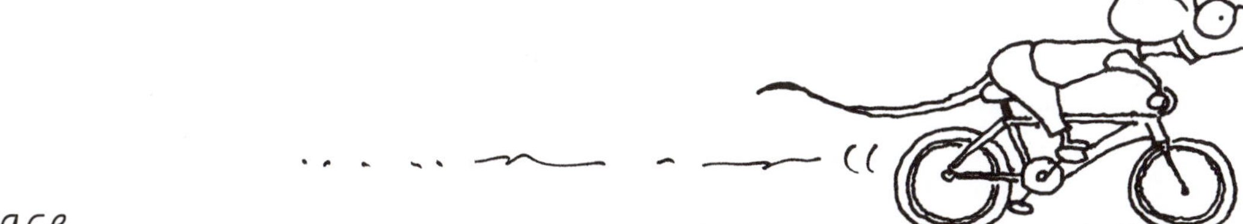

Trace.

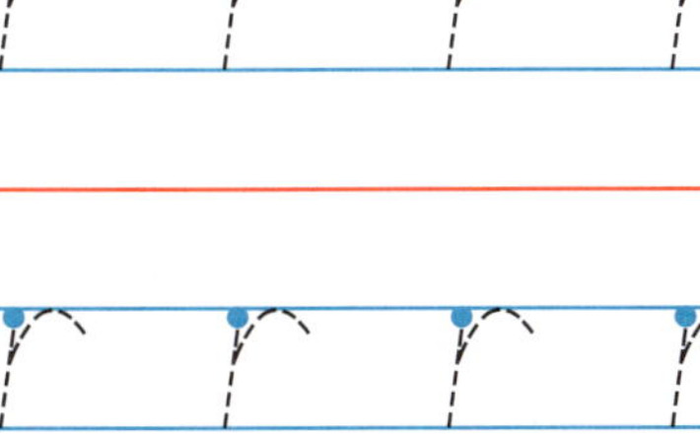

Write.

Patter

Slope down then retrace up, over the top and finish with a small downward stroke. Keep your pencil on the page.

Phonic chant

jiggly jellyfish

j j j

Trace the pattern.

Trace the pattern. Keep your pencil on the page.

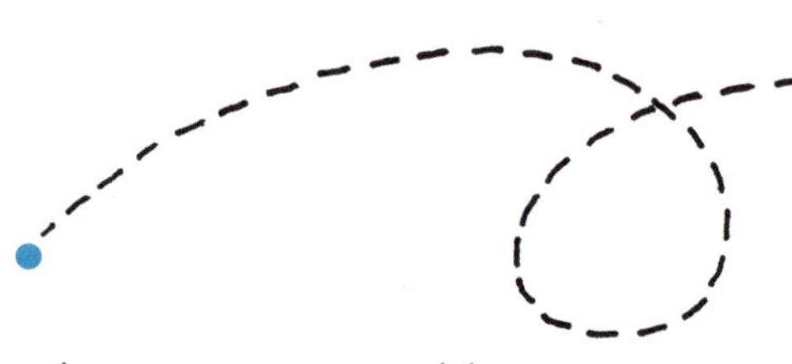

Trace the pattern. Keep your pencil on the page.

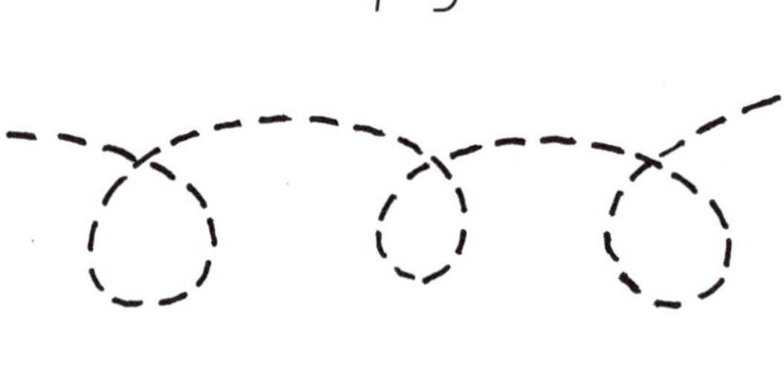

Track.

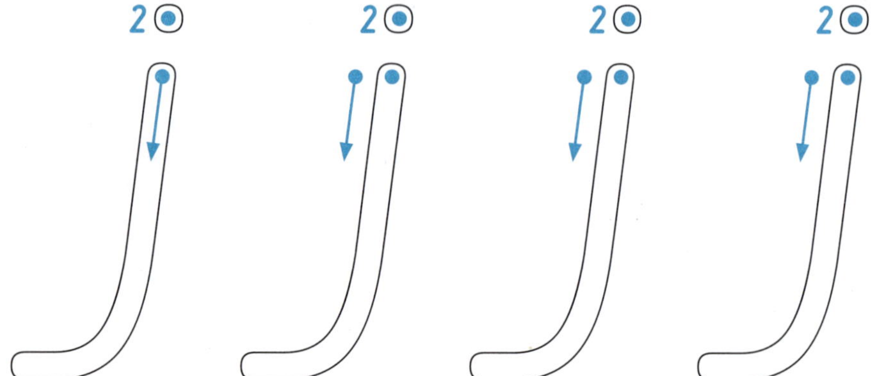
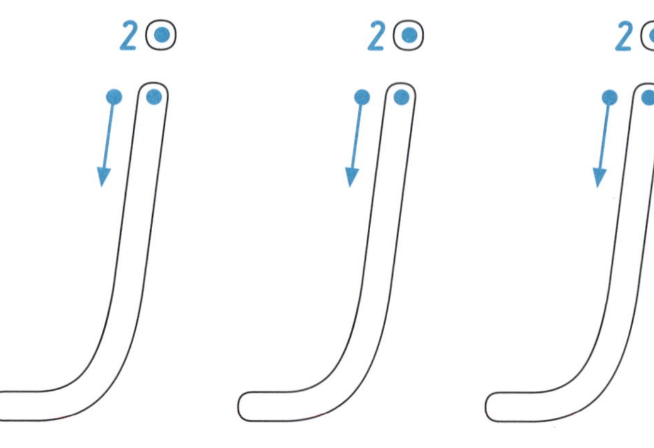

Handwriting: clockwise letter; body and tail letter (descender) (j).
Vocabulary: jiggly, jellyfish, jump.
Phonic knowledge /j/: jam, job, jet, jog.

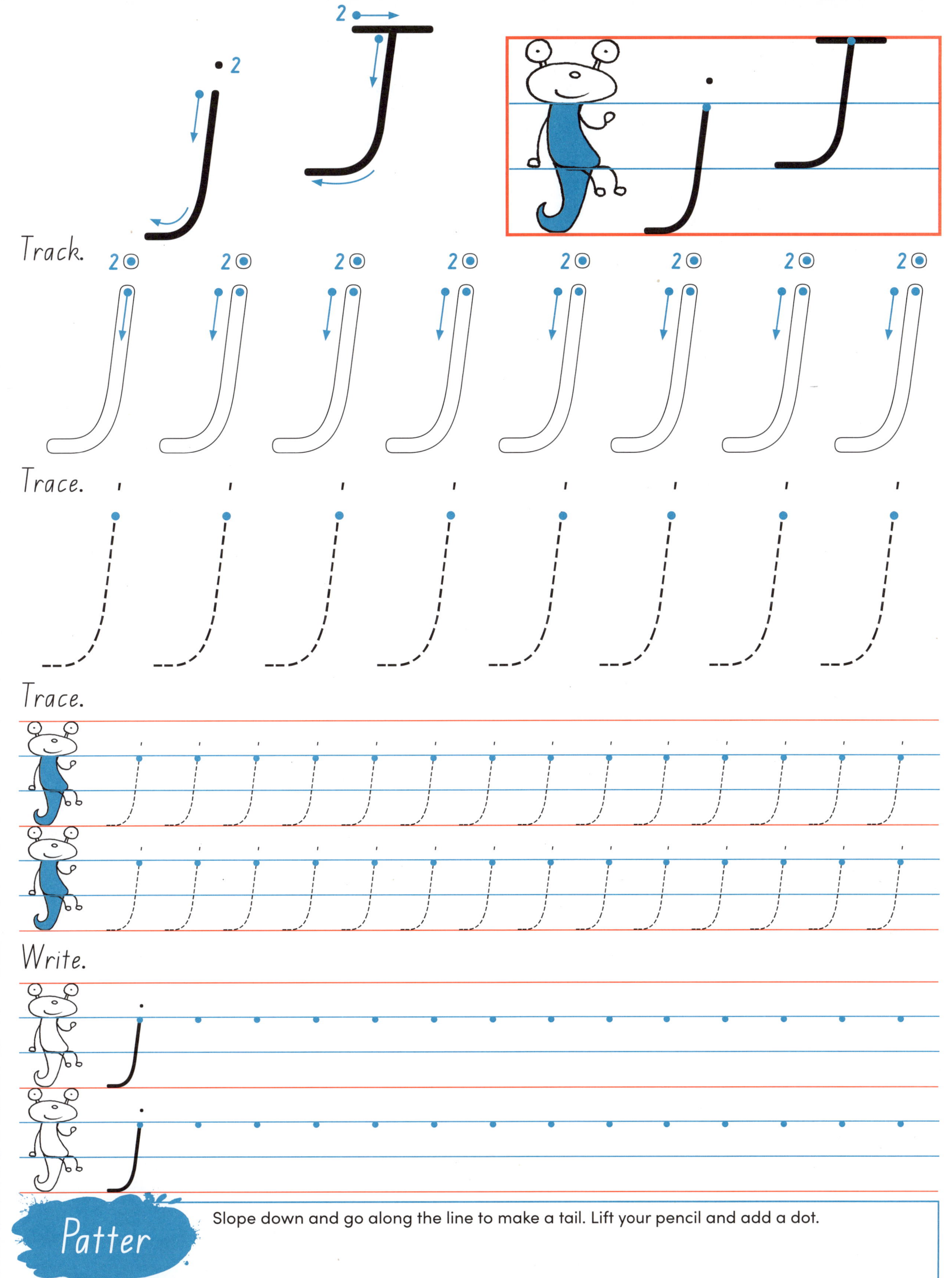
Track.
Trace.
Trace.
Write.
Patter
Slope down and go along the line to make a tail. Lift your pencil and add a dot.

Phonic chant

itchy iguana

i i i

Trace the pattern.

Trace.

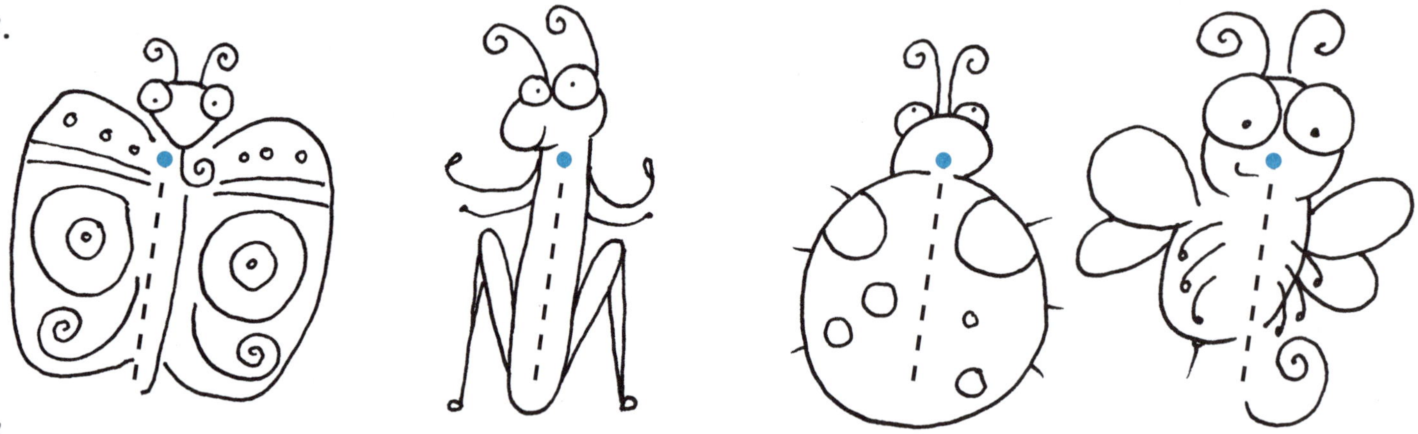

Trace.

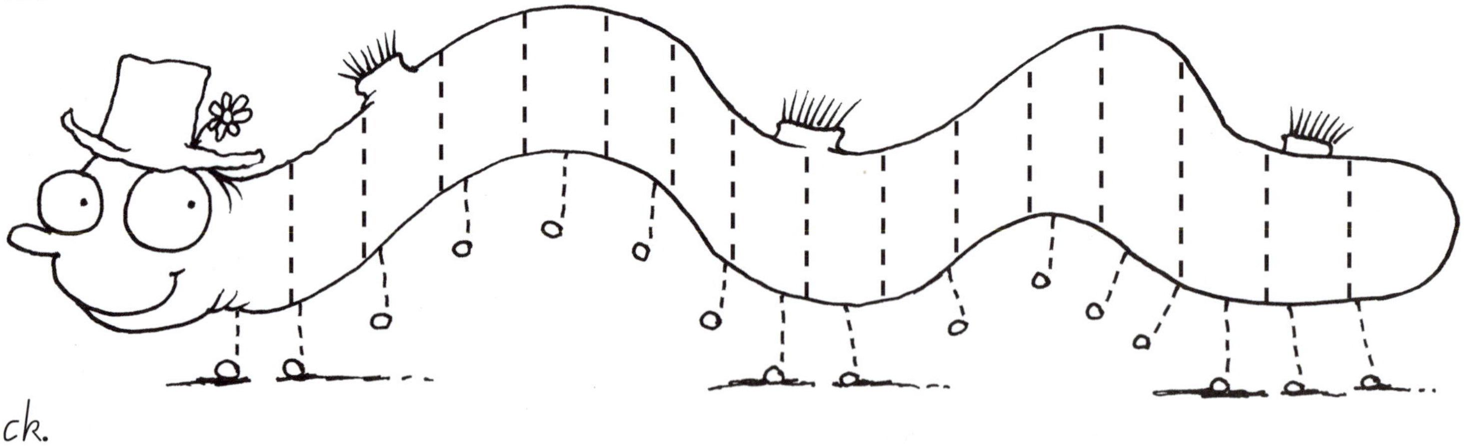

Track.

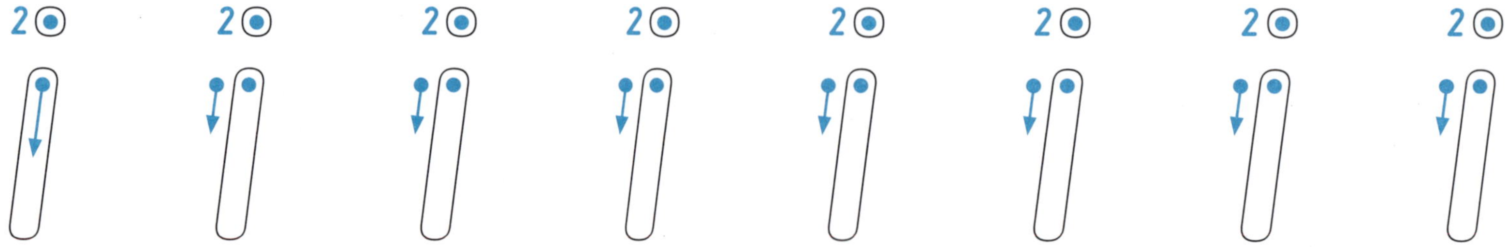

2 2 2 2 2 2 2 2

Handwriting: straight-line letter; body letter (i).
Vocabulary: itchy, iguana, insect, will.
Phonic knowledge /i/: is, it, if, in, six, sit, lip, pit, tip.

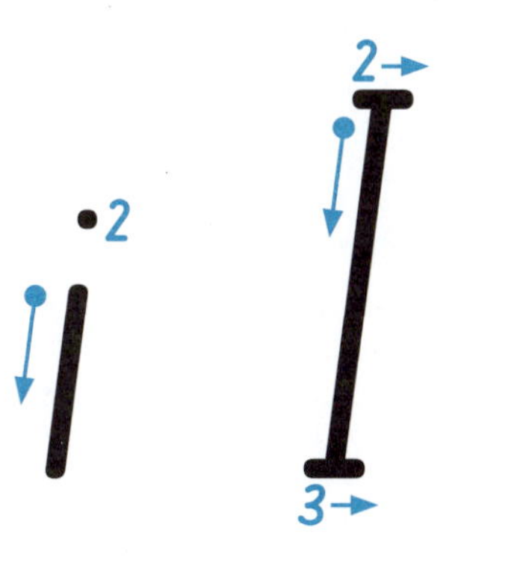

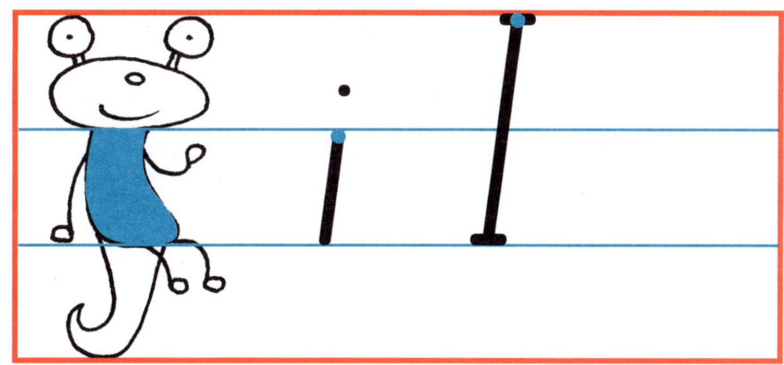

Trace the pattern. Keep your pencil on the page.

Copy the pattern.

illi

Trace.

Write.

i

i

Patter

Slope down. Lift your pencil and add a dot.

Phonic chant

tidy turtle

t t t

Trace the pattern.

Find and write t.

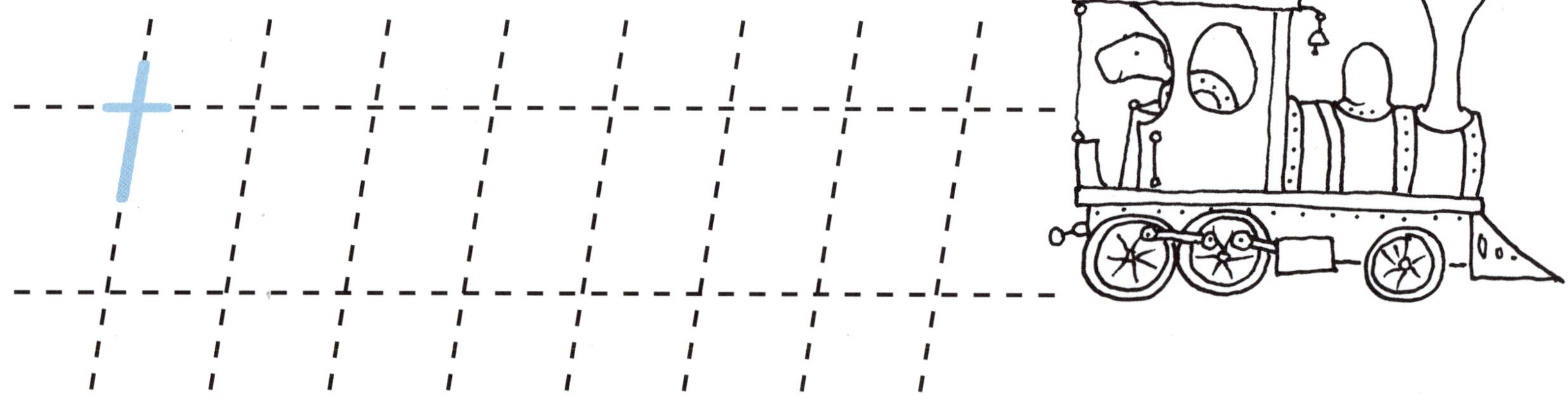

Track.

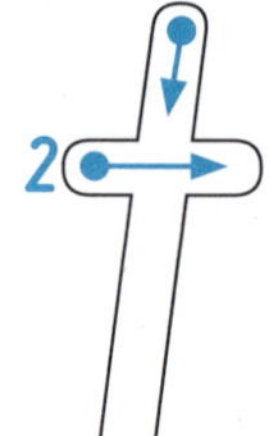

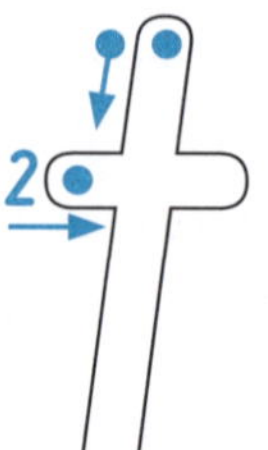

Handwriting: straight-line letter; head and body letter (ascender) (t).
Vocabulary: tidy, turtle, track, train, tree, tortoise.
Phonic knowledge /t/: tap, tip, ten, it, sit, at, sat, pat, hot, get, pet, net.

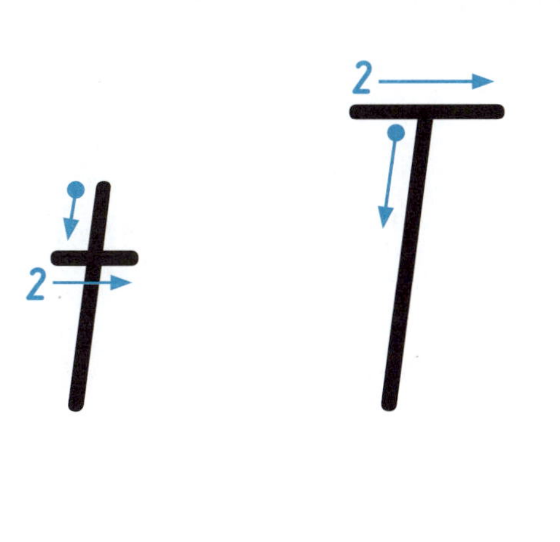

Track.

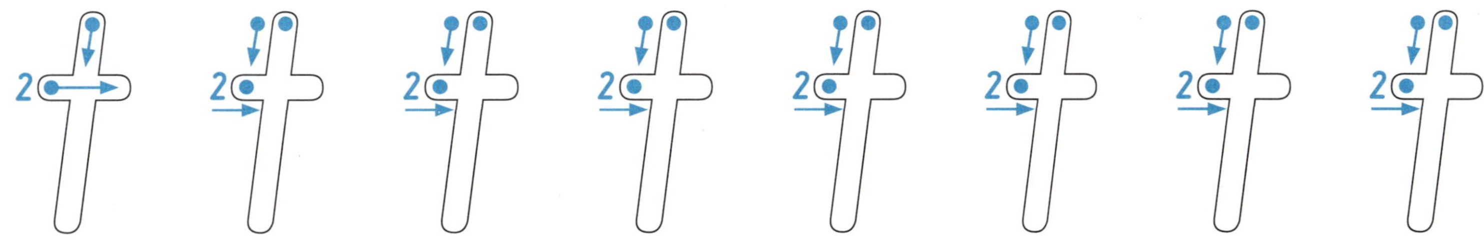

Trace.

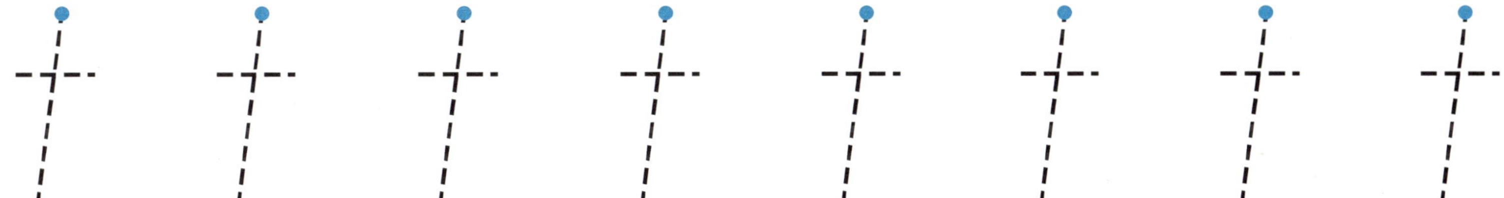

Trace.

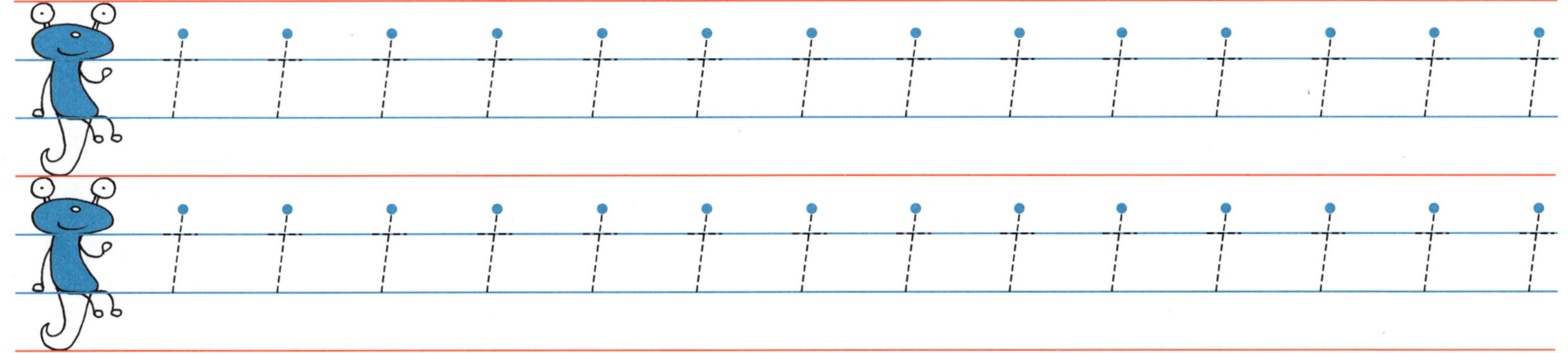

Write.

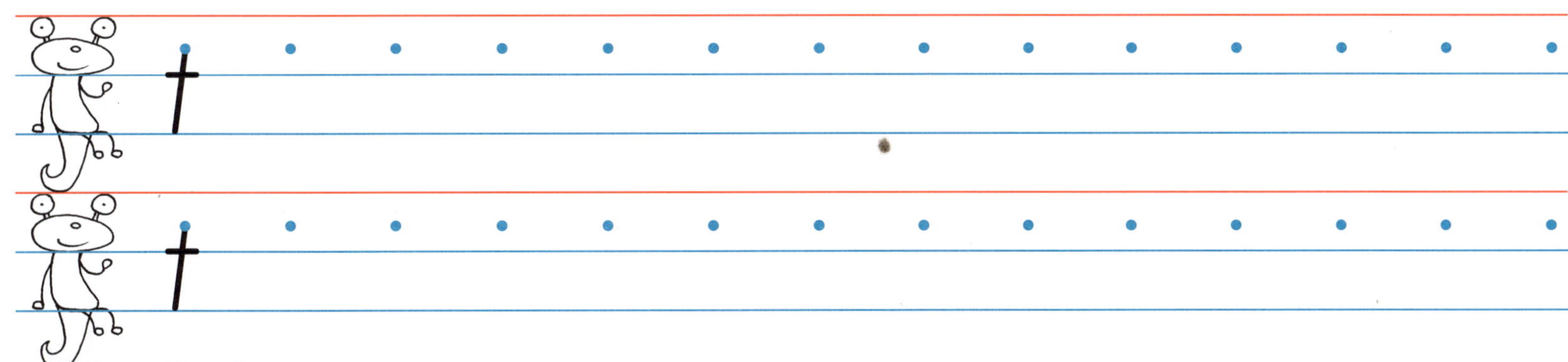

Patter

Start half way between the lines. Slope down. Lift your pencil and make a cross.

Phonic chant

lazy lion

l l l

Trace the pattern.

Trace the pattern.

Track.

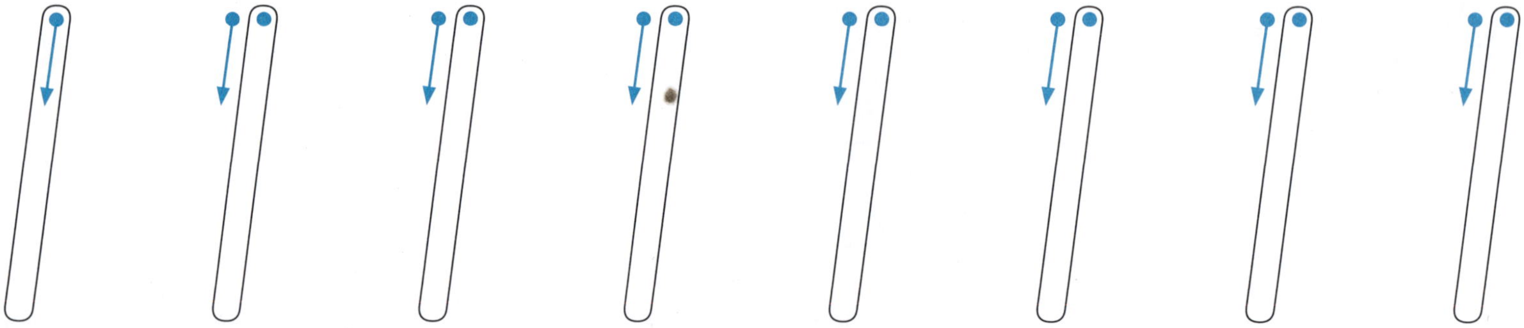

Handwriting: straight-line letter; head and body letter (ascender) (l).
Vocabulary: lazy, lion, love, light, little, like, laptop.
Phonic knowledge /l/: lap, let, lot, lit, leg, land, lump, bell, fill, tell.

Trace.
Trace.
Write.
Patter
Start at the very top and slope down. Keep your pencil on the page.

Phonic chant

foxy ox

x x x

Track the pattern.

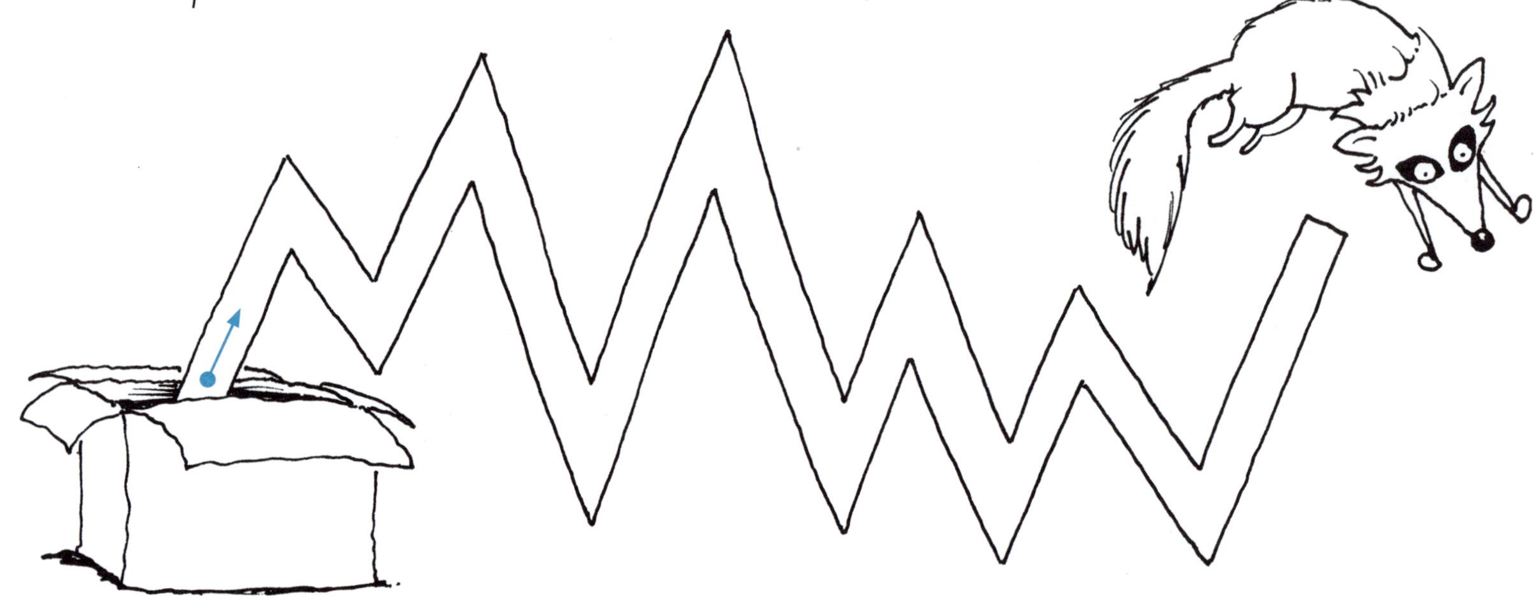

Trace the pattern. Find and write x.

Track.

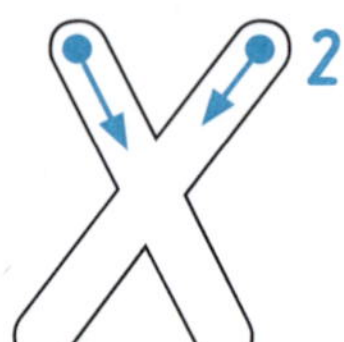
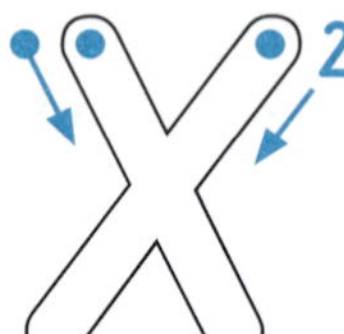
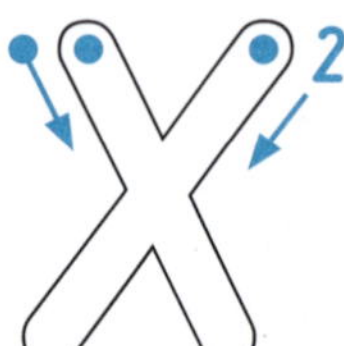
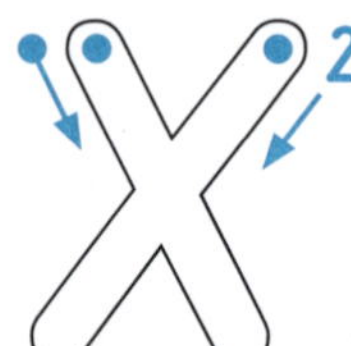
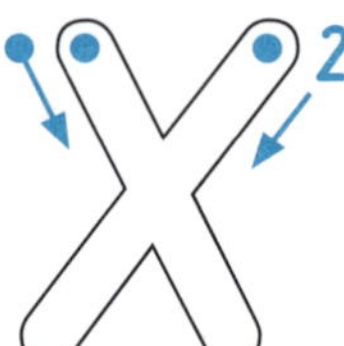
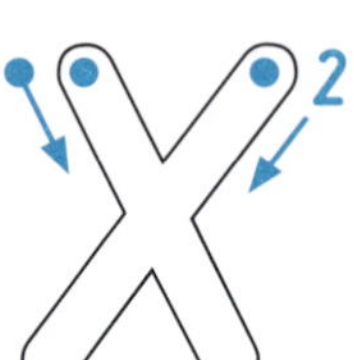

Handwriting: straight-line letter; body letter (x).
Vocabulary: x-ray.
Phonic knowledge /ks/: mix, fix, box, six, fox, ox.

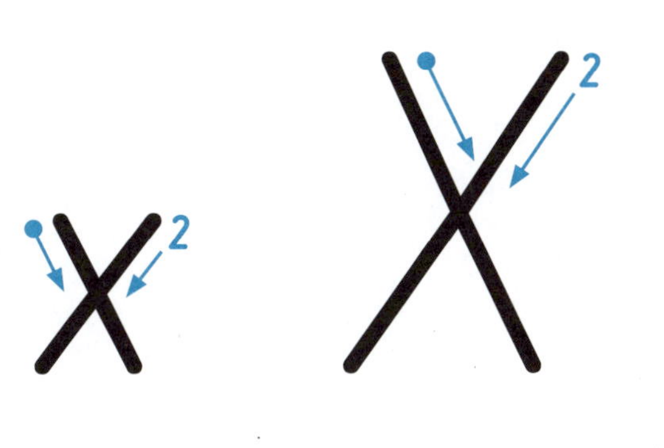

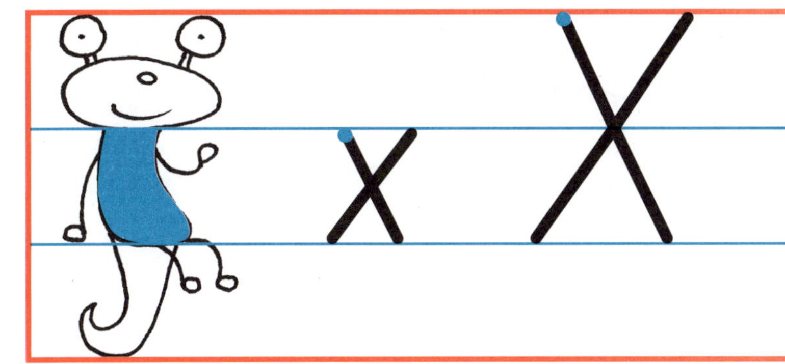

Track.

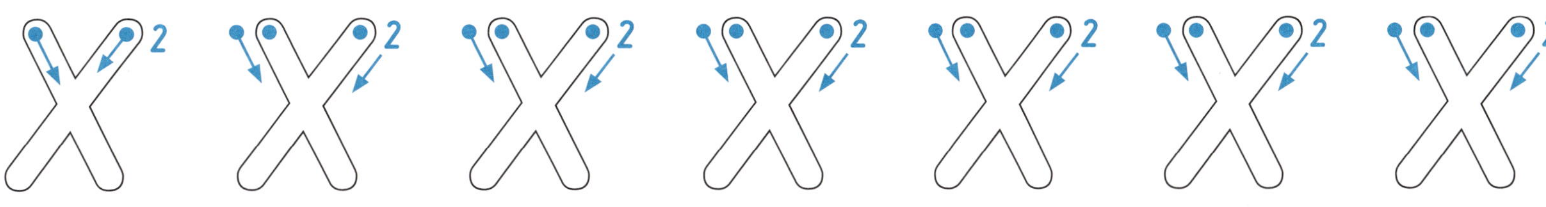

Trace.

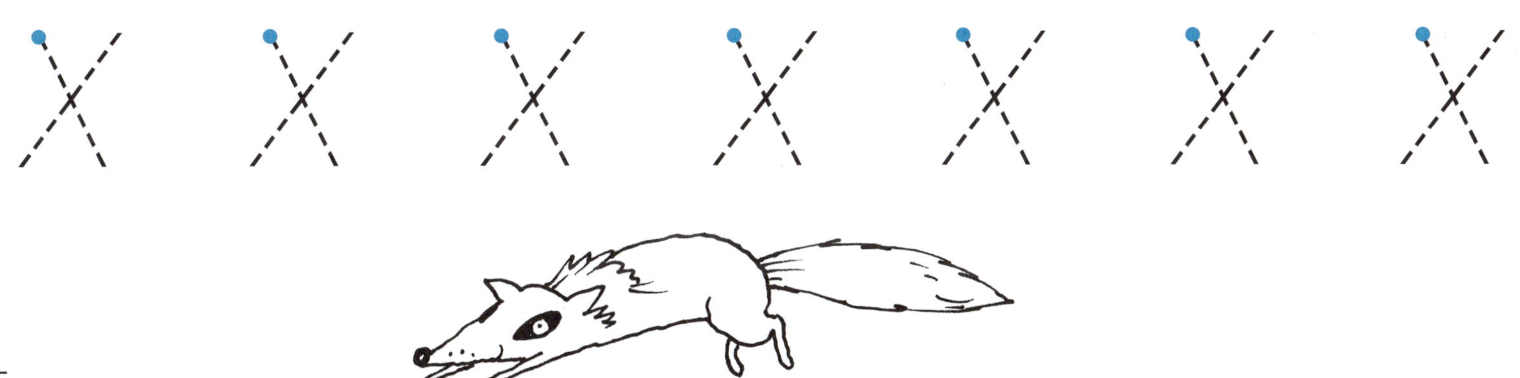

Trace.

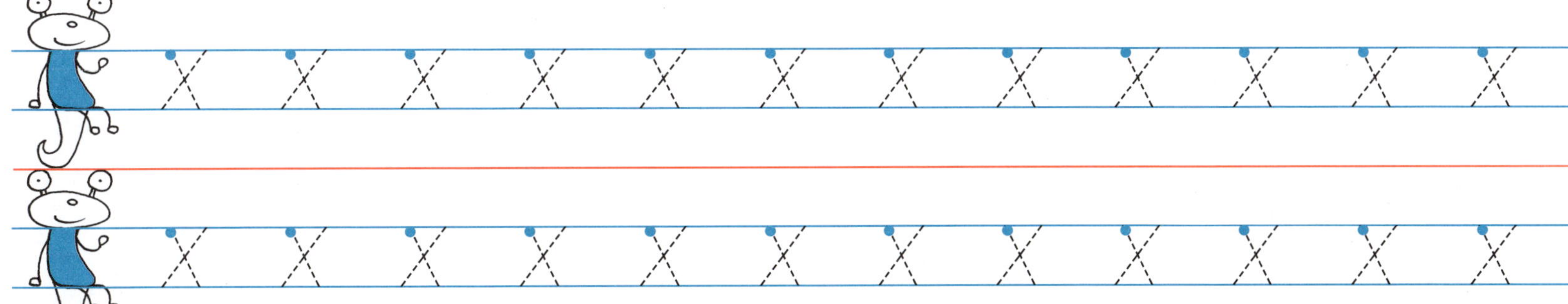

Write.

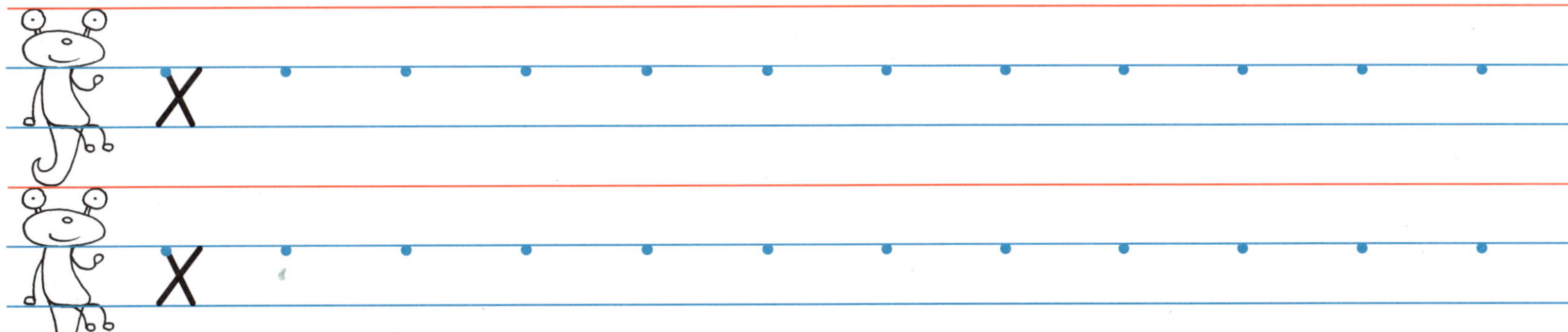

Patter

Make a straight stroke. Lift your pencil and cross it with another straight stroke.

Phonic chant

zigzag zebra

z z z

Trace the pattern.

Trace the pattern.

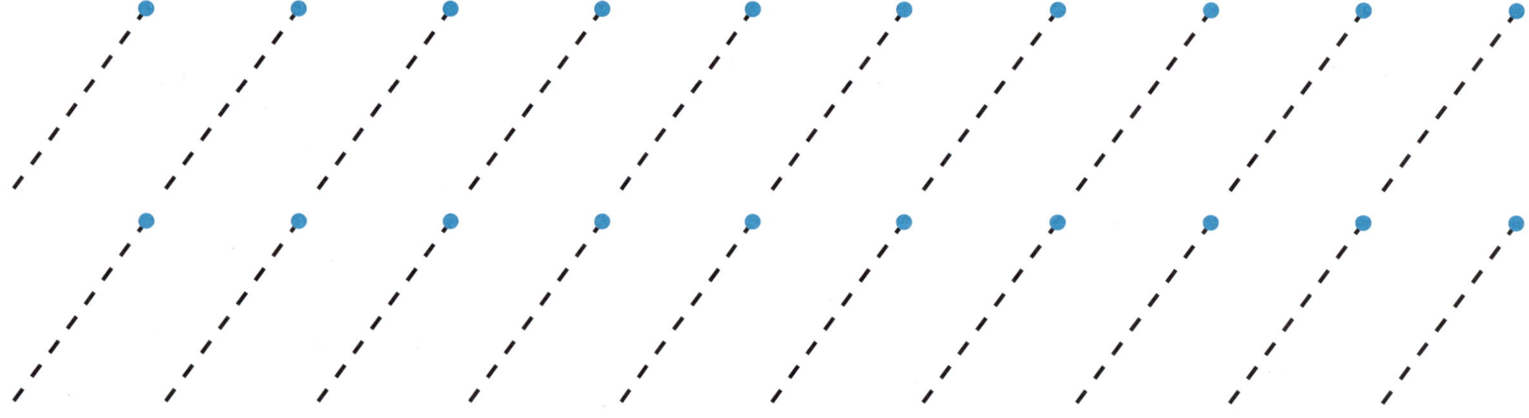

Find z.

Track.

Handwriting: straight-line letter; body letter (z).
Vocabulary: zigzag, zebra, zoo, pizza, zipper.
Phonic knowledge /z/: zip, zap, buzz, jazz, fizz.

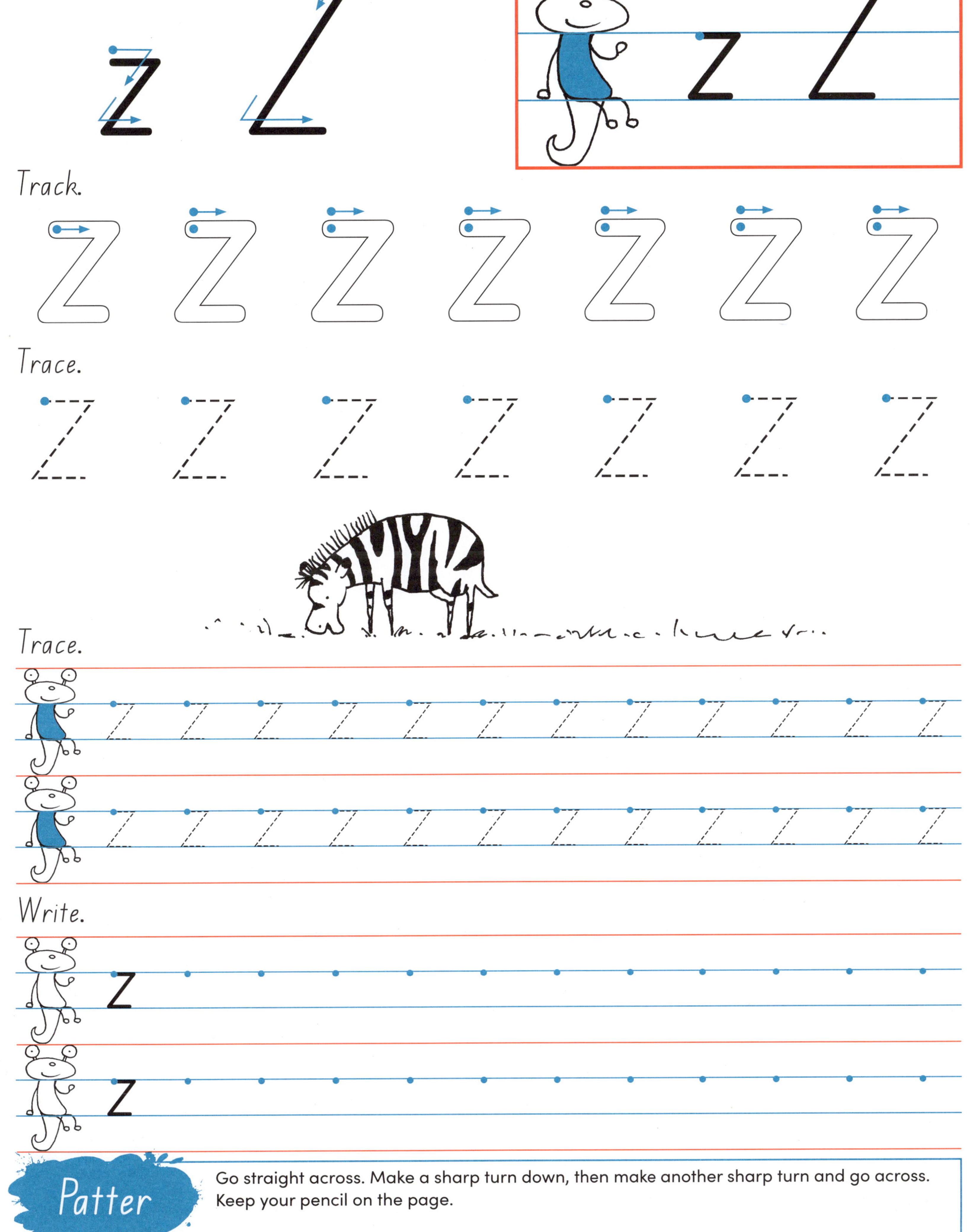

Patter

Go straight across. Make a sharp turn down, then make another sharp turn and go across. Keep your pencil on the page.

Phonic chant

ugly undies

u u u

Trace the pattern.

Find u.

u

Trace the pattern. Keep your pencil on the page.

Track.

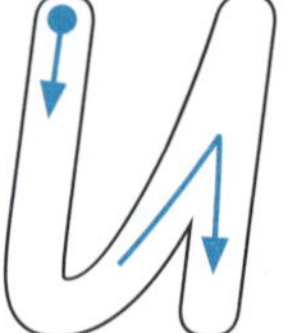

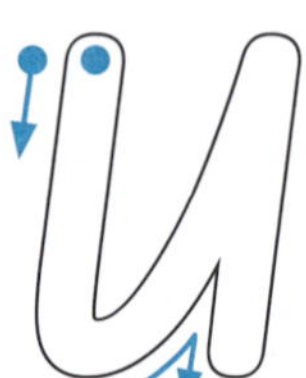
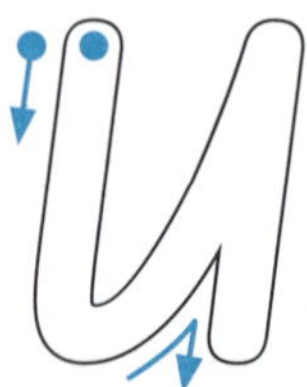

Handwriting: anticlockwise letter; body letter (u).
Vocabulary: ugly, undies, umbrella, under, shut.
Phonic knowledge /u/: up, mum, bug, but, mug, cup, duck, sunset.

Track.

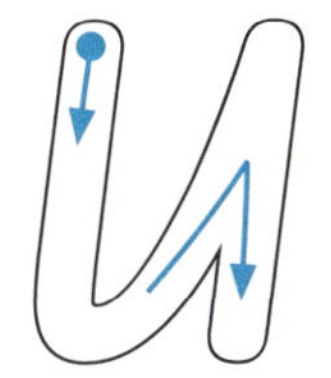  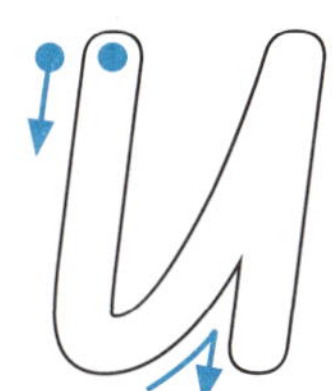 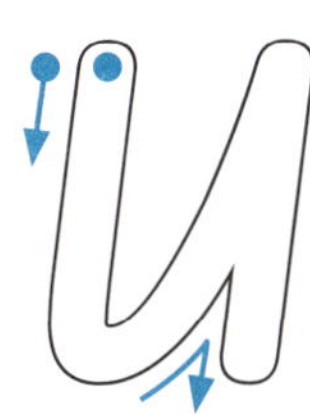  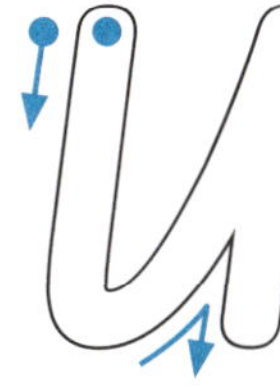

Trace.

  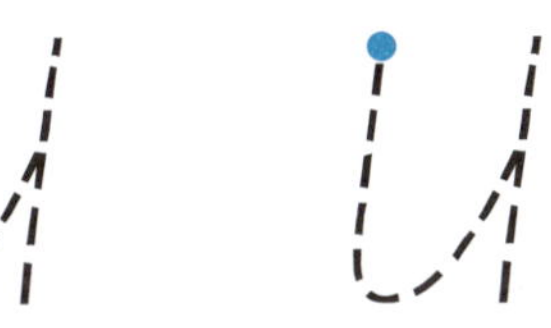 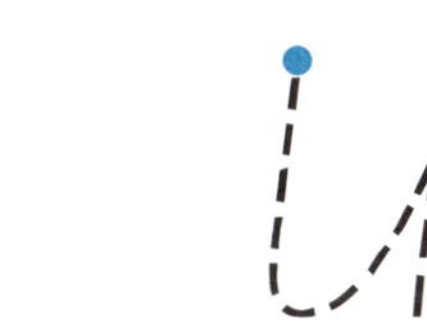  

Trace.

 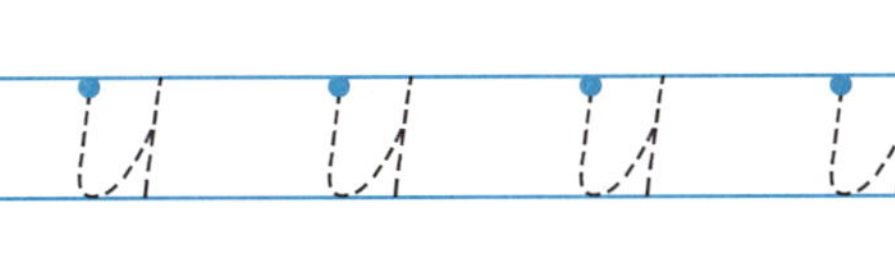 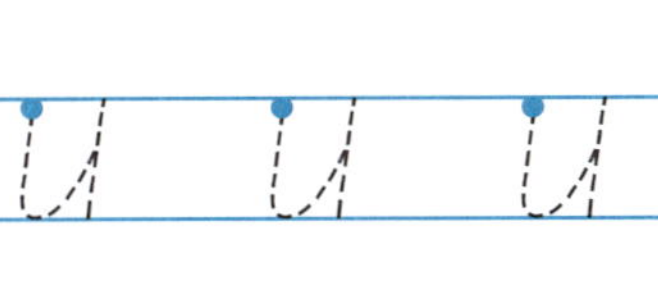 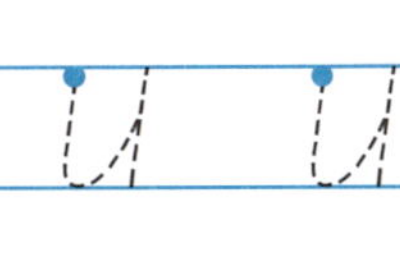 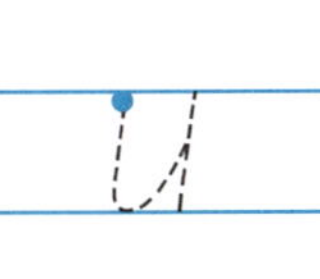 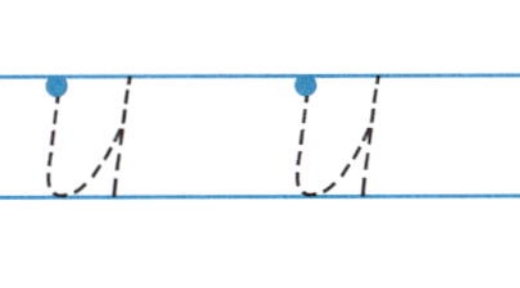

Write.

 u

 u

Patter

Go down, around, up and down. Keep your pencil on the page.

Phonic chant

vicious vulture

v v v

Trace the pattern.

Trace the pattern. Keep your pencil on the page.

Trace the pattern. Turn each pattern into a picture.

Track.

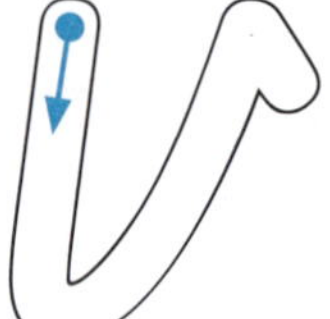

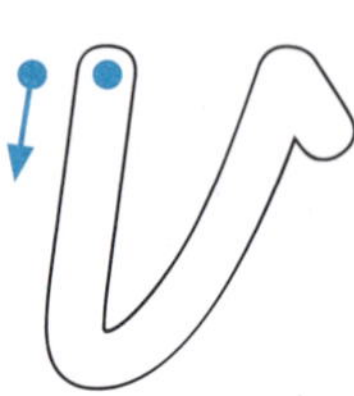

Handwriting: anticlockwise letter; body letter (v).
Vocabulary: violin, vulture, vicious.
Phonic knowledge /v/: vet, van, visit, very.

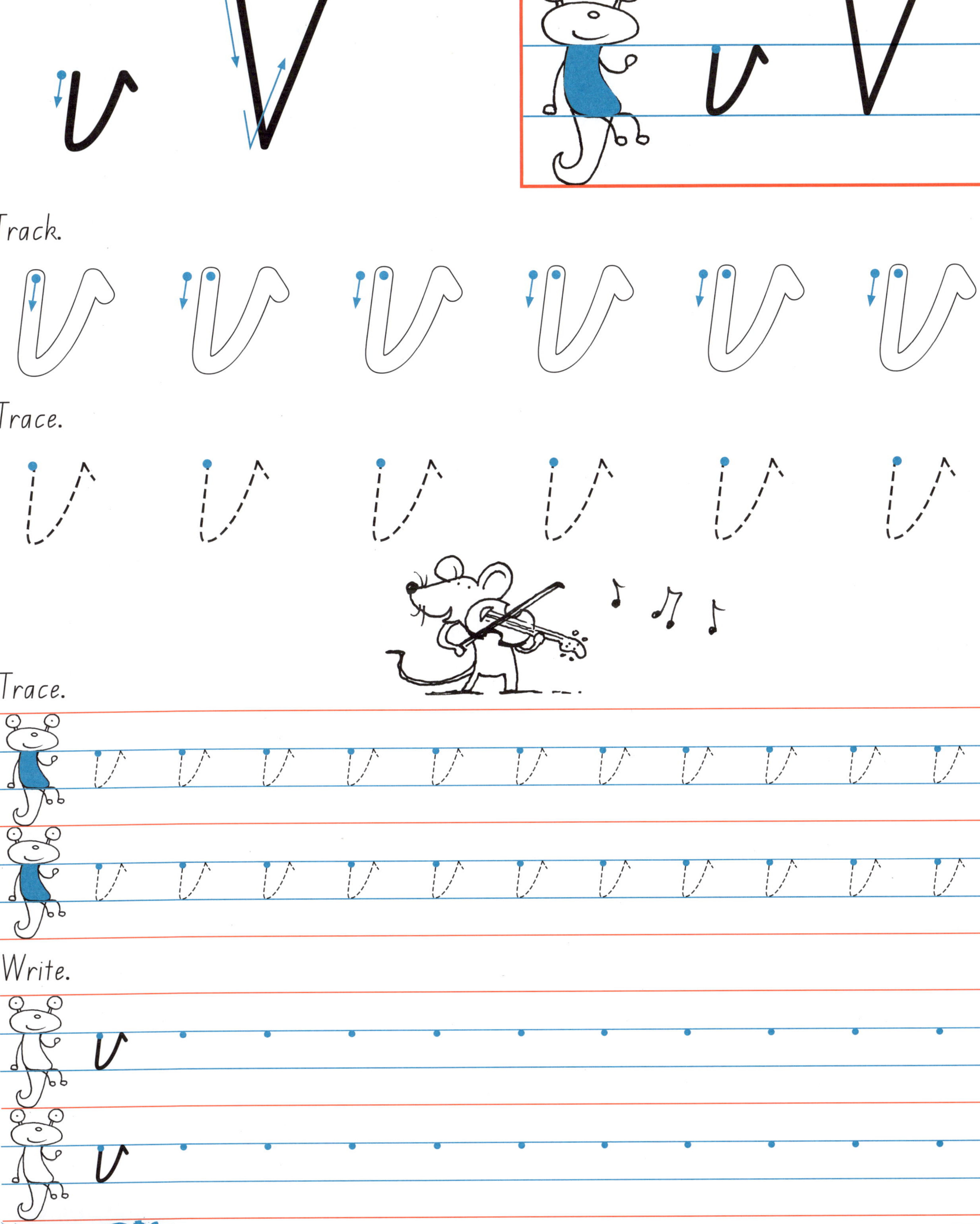

Patter

Go down, around and up, then exit with a short stroke. Keep your pencil on the page.

Phonic chant

wiggly wolf

w w w

Trace the pattern.

Trace the pattern. Keep your pencil on the page.

Trace the pattern. Turn each pattern into a picture.

Track.

Handwriting: anticlockwise letter; body letter (w).
Vocabulary: wiggly, wings, wolf, whale, wish, when, where, why.
Phonic knowledge /w/: wet, win, we, web, went, want, was.

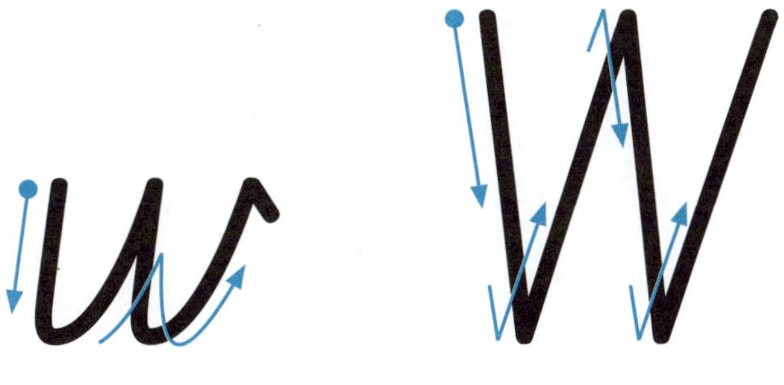

Track.

Trace.

Trace.

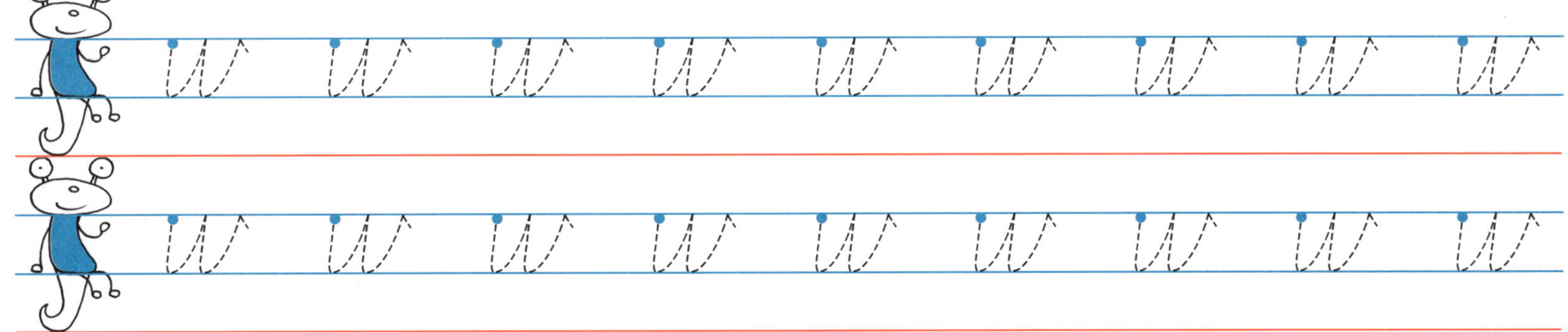

Write.

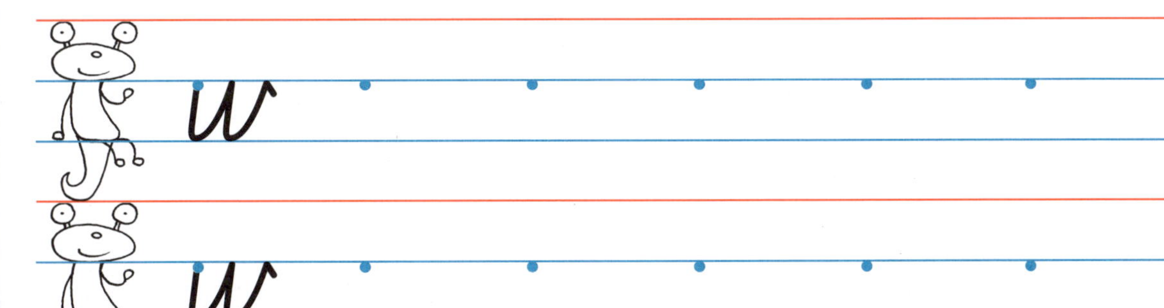

Patter

Go down, around, up then down again, around and up, then exit with a short stroke. Keep your pencil on the page.

Phonic chant

angry alligator
a a a

Track the pattern. Keep your pencil on the page.

Trace the pattern. Keep your pencil on the page.

Trace the pattern.

Track.

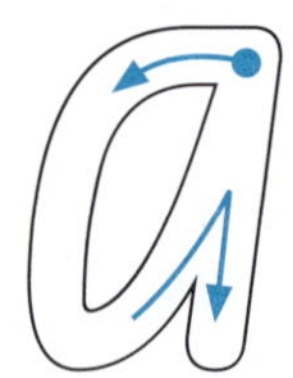     

Handwriting: anticlockwise letter; body letter (a).
Vocabulary: anteater, angry, alligator, apple.
Phonic knowledge /a/: an, ant, cat, mat, sat, tap, pat.

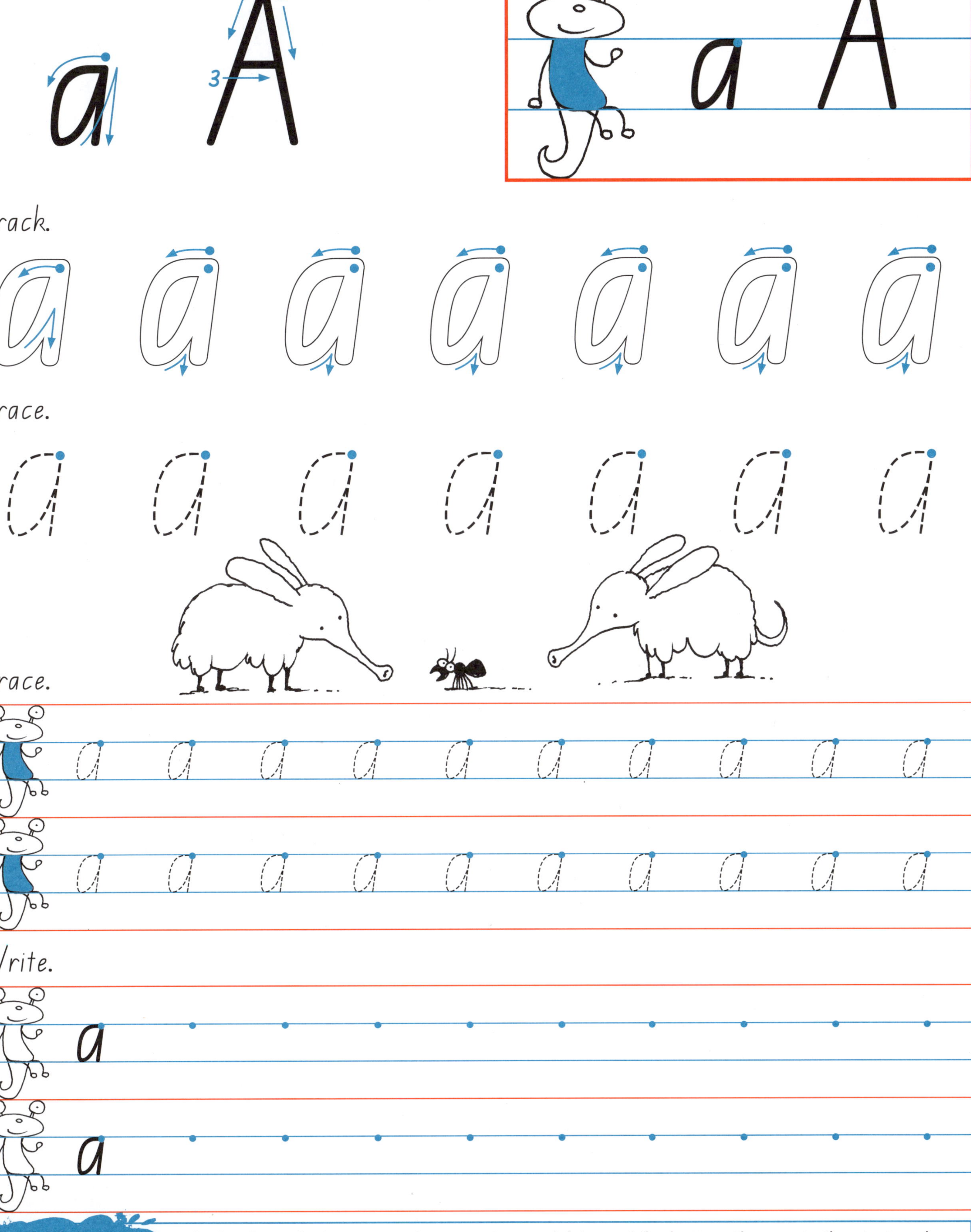

Patter

Go backwards then curve down, make a quick turn at the bottom then up to the start and drop down. Keep your pencil on the page.

Phonic chant

dirty dingo
d d d

Trace the pattern.

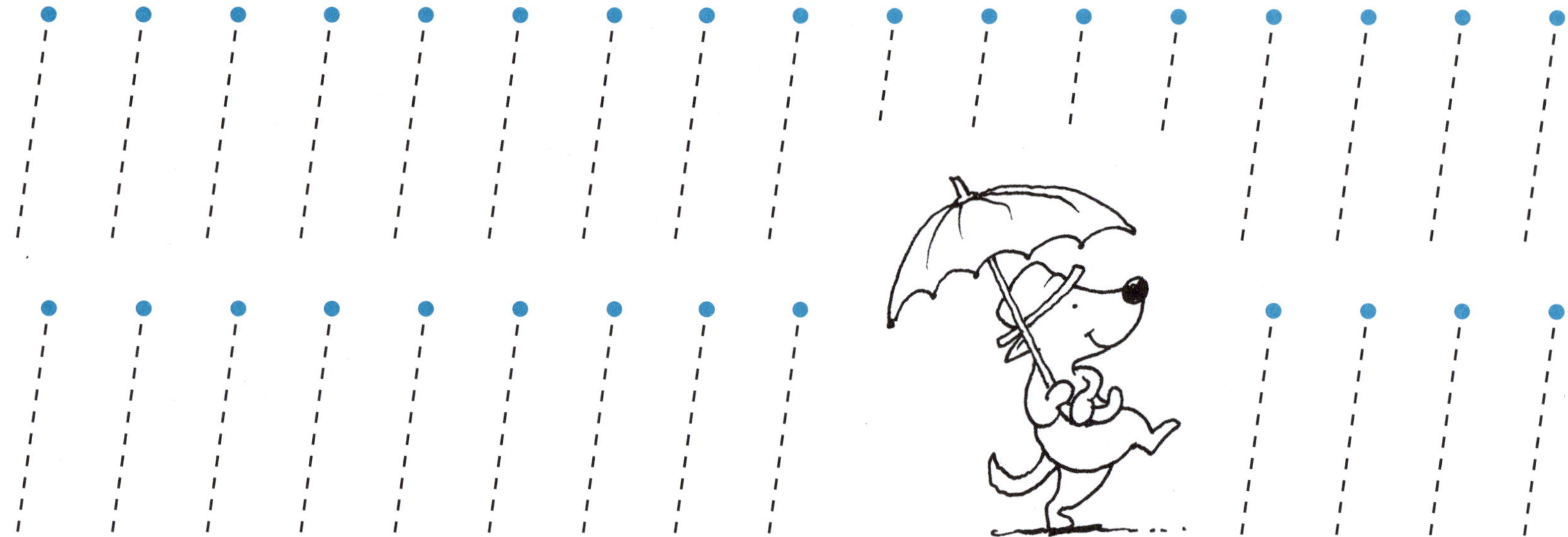

Trace the pattern.

Track.

Handwriting: anticlockwise letter; head and body letter (ascender) (d). **Vocabulary:** dingo, dirty, down.
The word *dingo* is based on the word *dingu* from the Dharug and Dharawal languages. It means 'wild dog'.
Phonic knowledge /d/: do, don't, dog, din, dip, dad, did, lid, and, mad, sad, sand, stand, said.

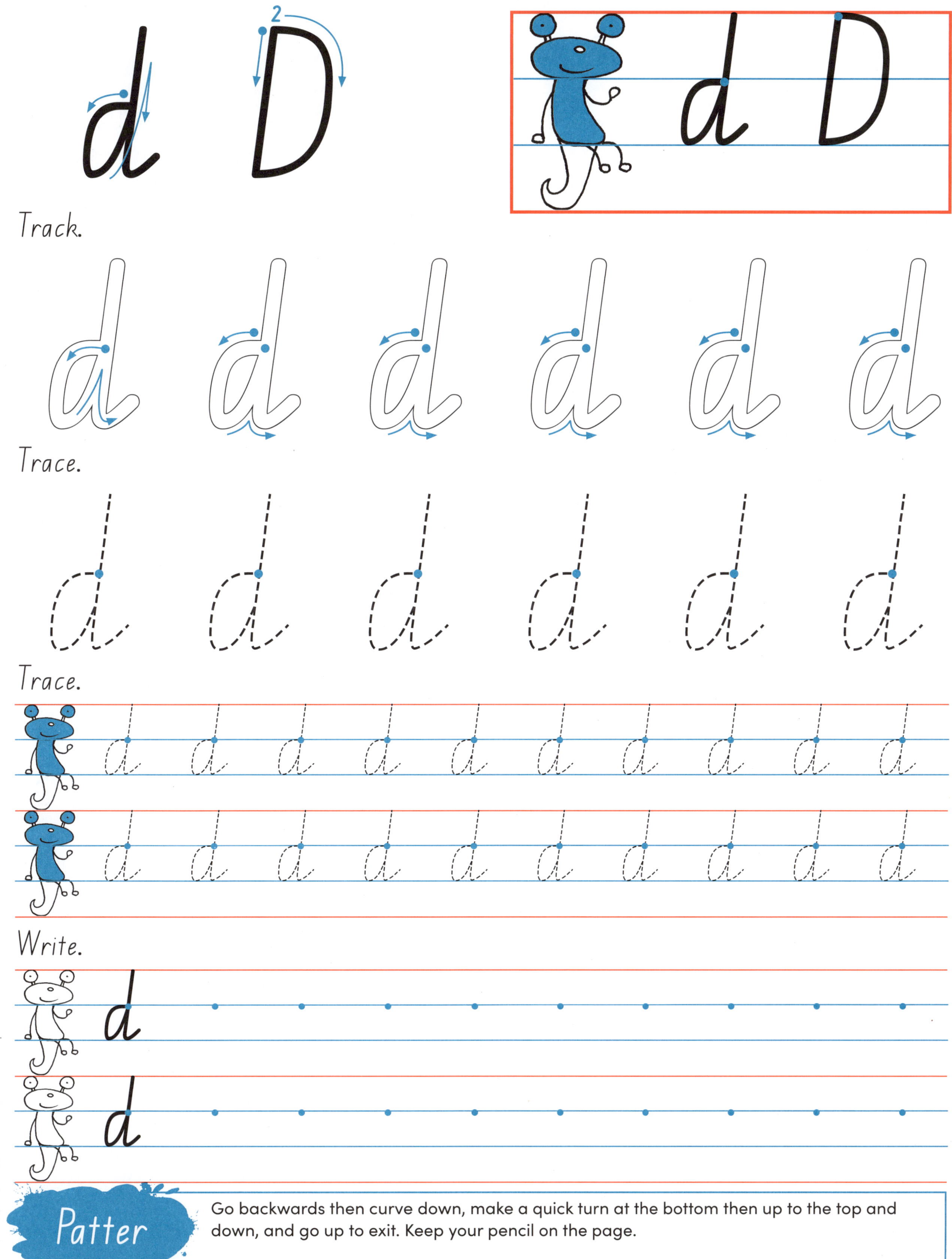

Patter

Go backwards then curve down, make a quick turn at the bottom then up to the top and down, and go up to exit. Keep your pencil on the page.

Phonic chant

quick quokkas
qu qu qu

Trace the pattern. Keep your pencil on the page.

Trace the pattern. Keep your pencil on the page.

Trace.

Track.

Handwriting: anticlockwise letter; body and tail letter (descender)
Vocabulary: quokka, queen. The word *quokka* is based on the word *gwagga* from the Noongar language.
Phonic knowledge /kw/: quick, quack, quiz.

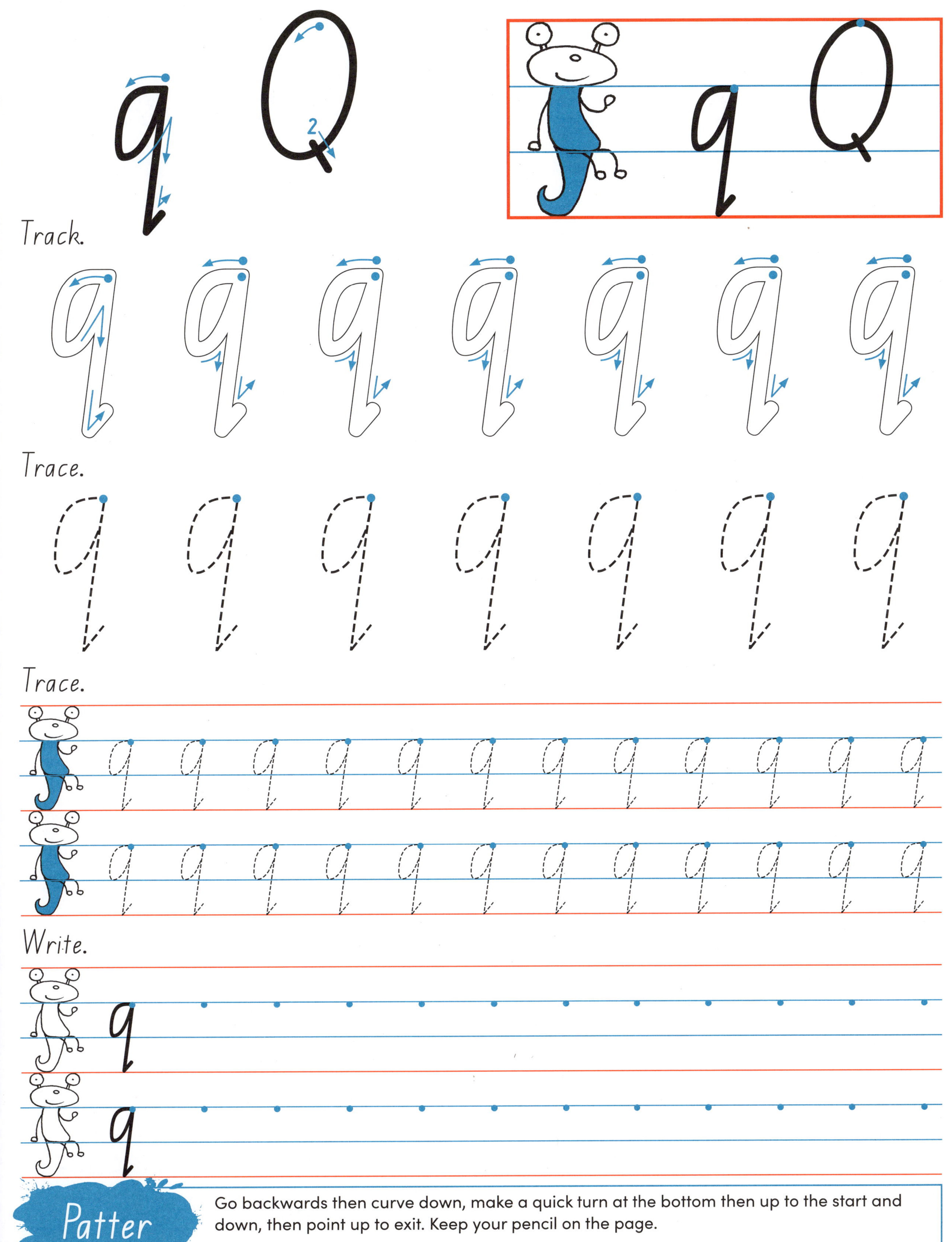

Patter

Go backwards then curve down, make a quick turn at the bottom then up to the start and down, then point up to exit. Keep your pencil on the page.

Phonic chant

orange octopus

o o o

Trace the pattern.

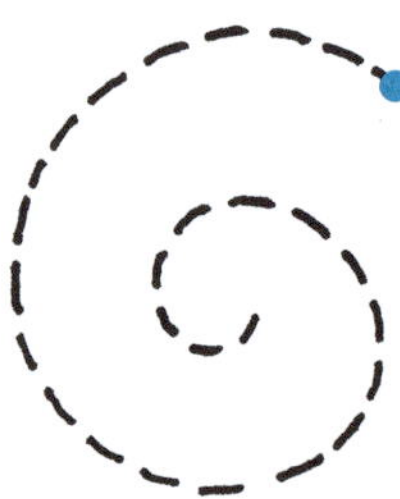 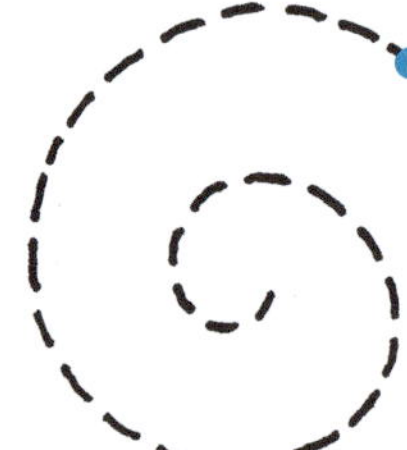 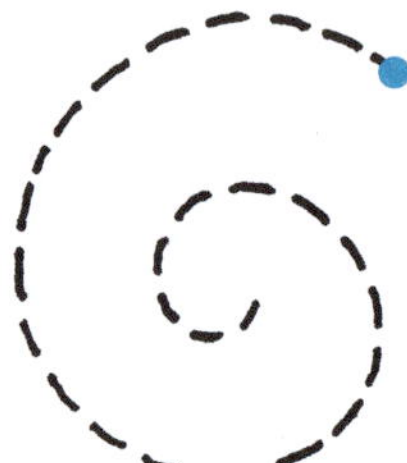 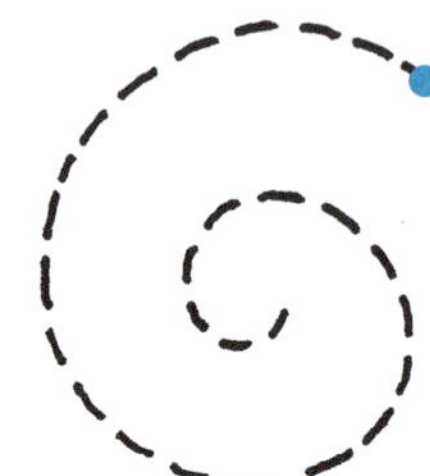 

Trace the pattern. Keep your pencil on the page.

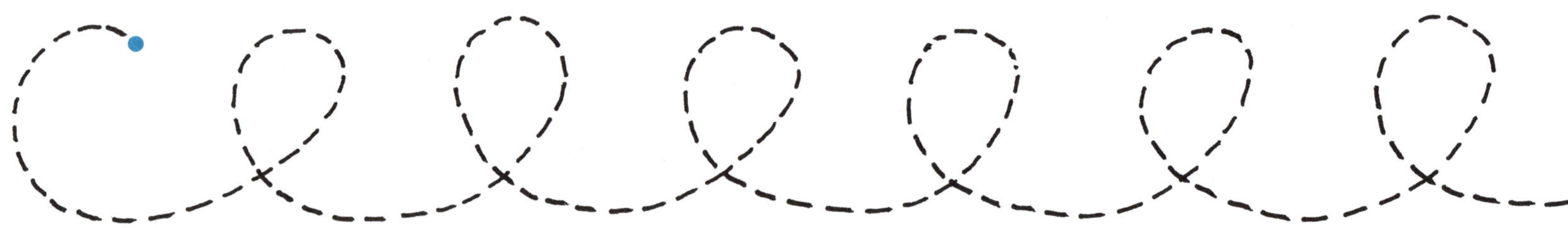

Trace the pattern.

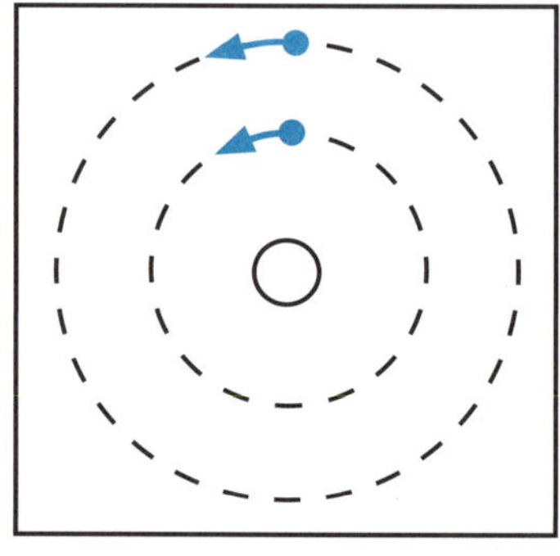 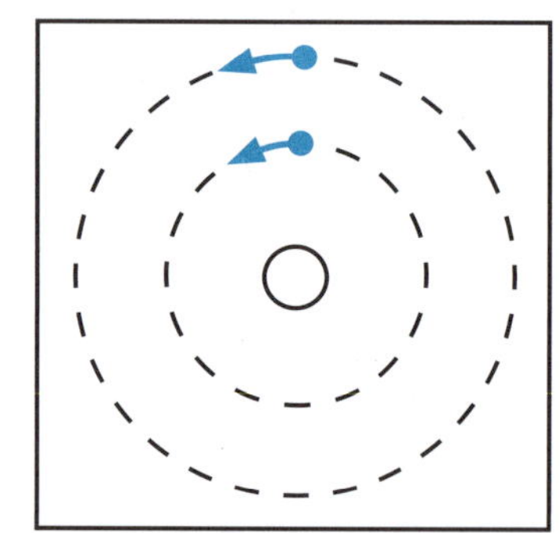 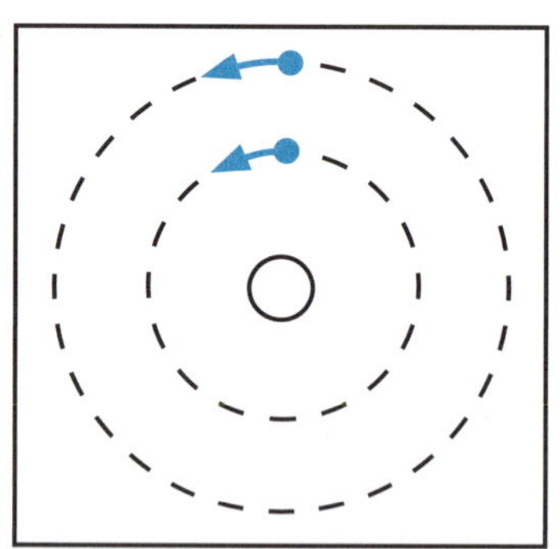 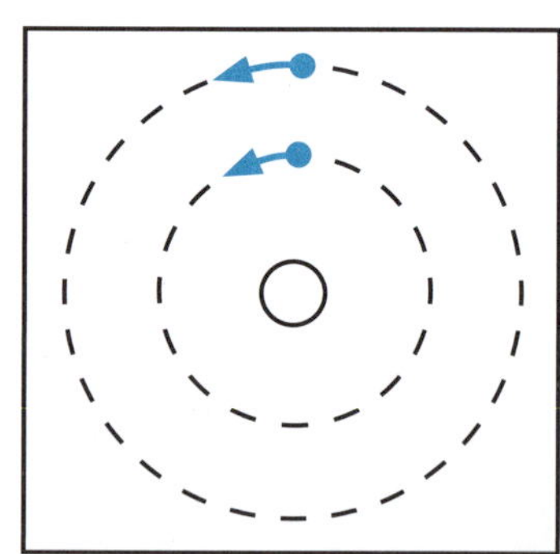

Track.

  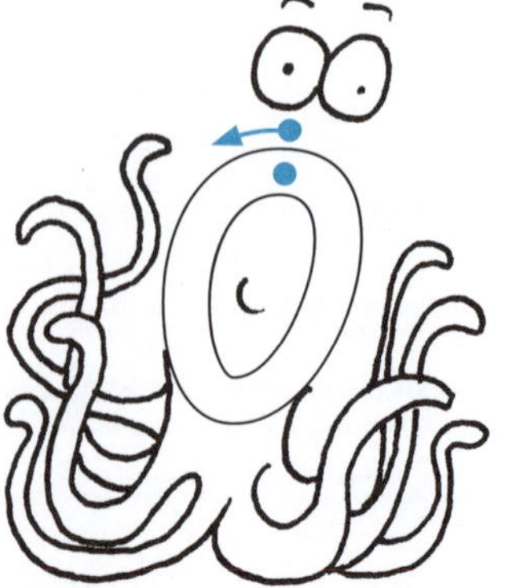 

Handwriting: anticlockwise letter; body letter (o).
Vocabulary: orange, octopus.
Phonic knowledge /o/: on, not, got, hot, pot, of, to, log, pop, top, mop, stop.

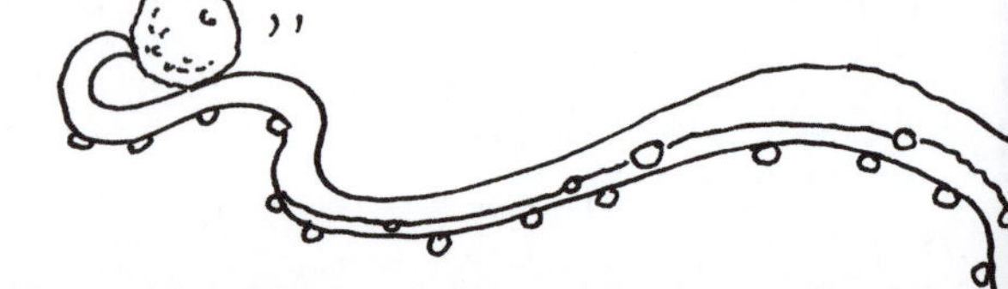

Track.

Trace.

Trace.

Write.

Patter

Start at 12 o'clock. Go backwards and curve down, around the bottom and up to join where you started. Keep your pencil on the page.

Phonic chant

energetic elephant

e e e

Trace the pattern. Keep your pencil on the page.

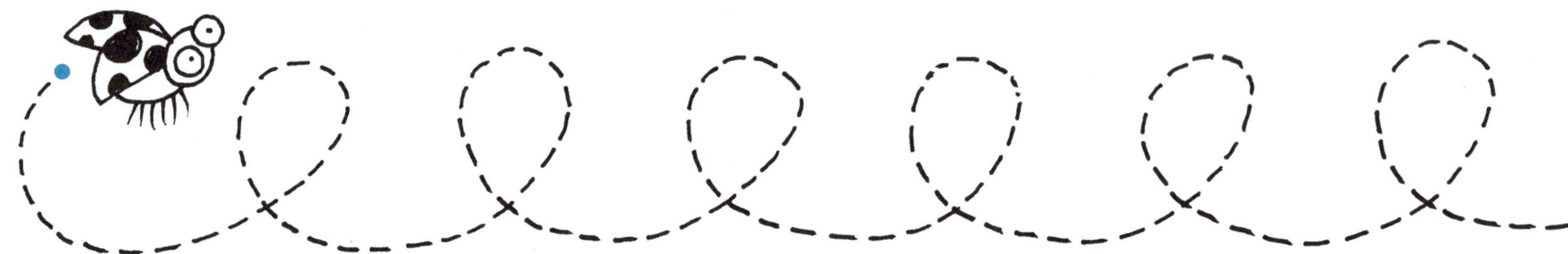

Trace the pattern.

Trace the pattern.

Track.

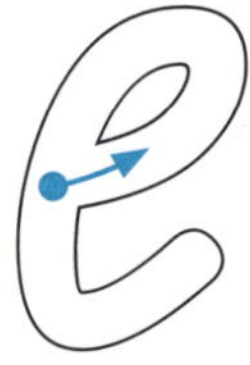

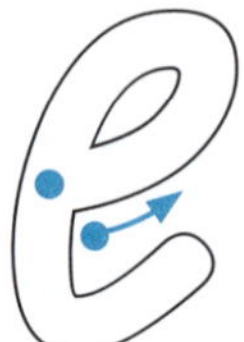

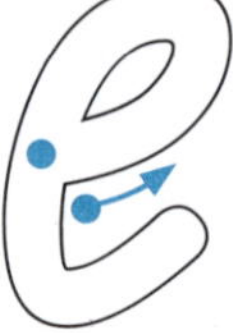

Handwriting: anticlockwise letter; body letter (e).
Vocabulary: elephant, energetic, eagle, eat, beetle, he, she, the.
Phonic knowledge /e/: egg, hen, men, ten, pen, met, net, get, red.

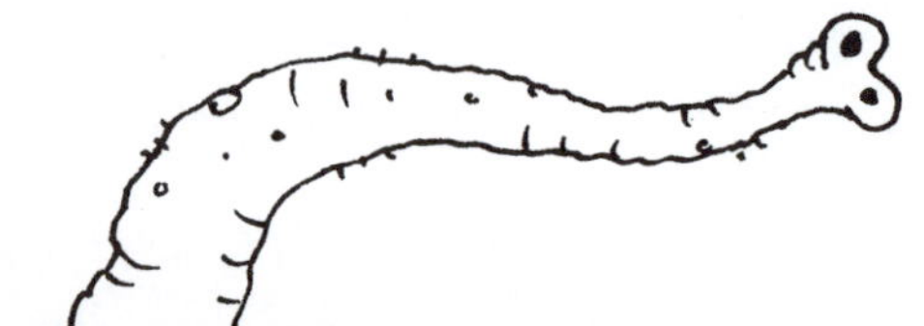

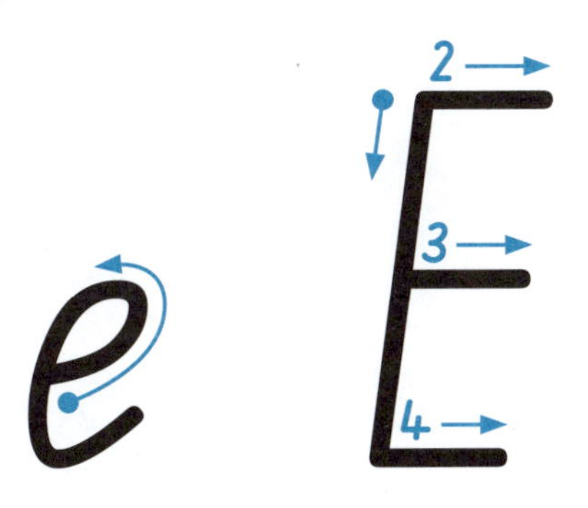

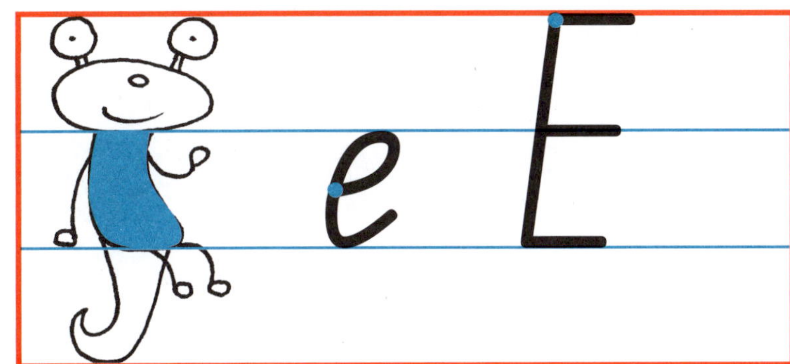

Track.

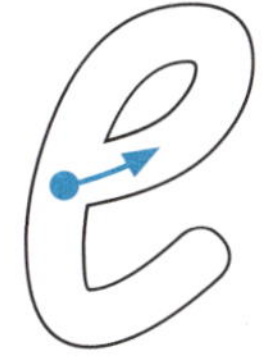   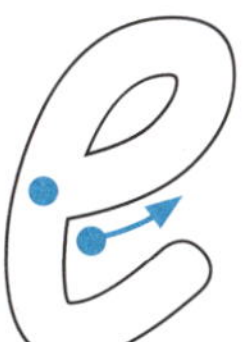 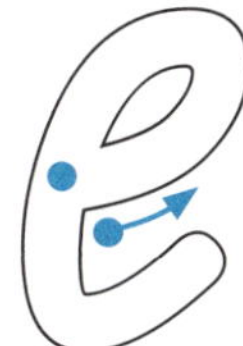 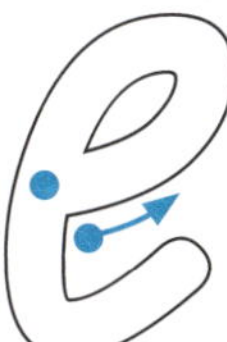 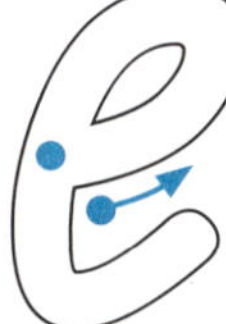

Trace.

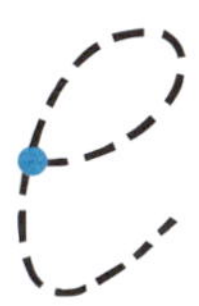    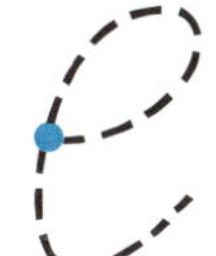 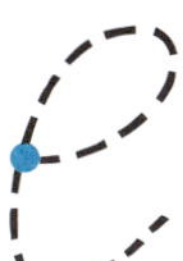 

Trace.

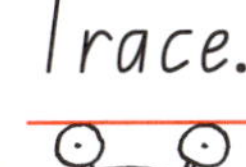

 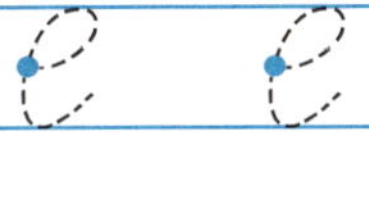 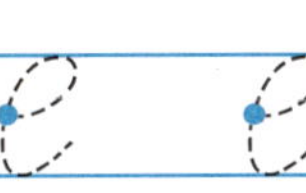 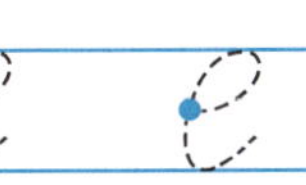  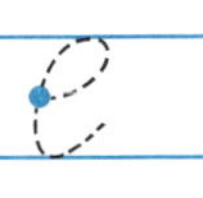   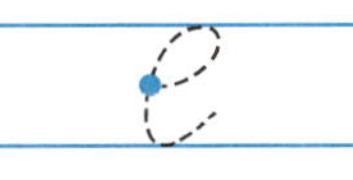

Write.

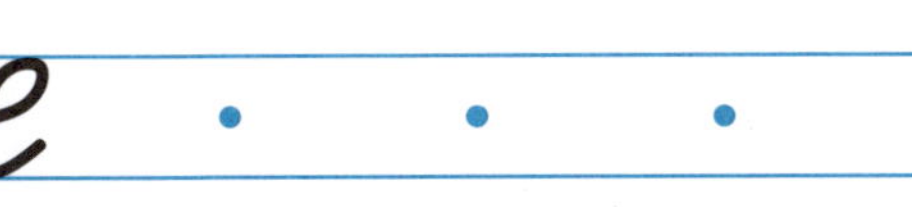     

Patter

Start in the middle, sweep up and make a smooth turn. Go around to end. Keep your pencil on the page.

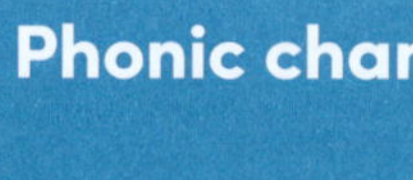

Phonic chant

cool cow

c c c

Trace the pattern.

Find c.

Track.

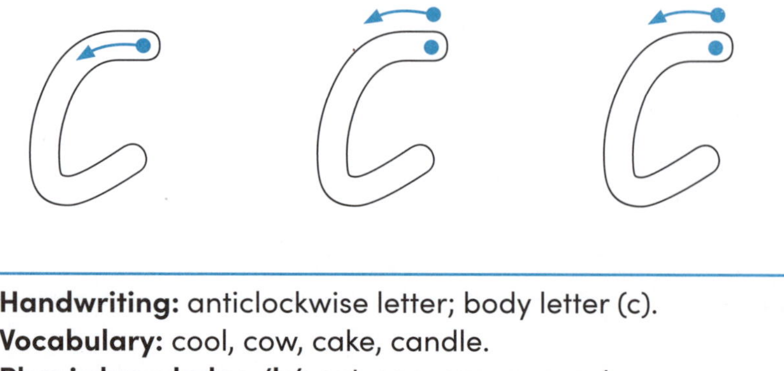

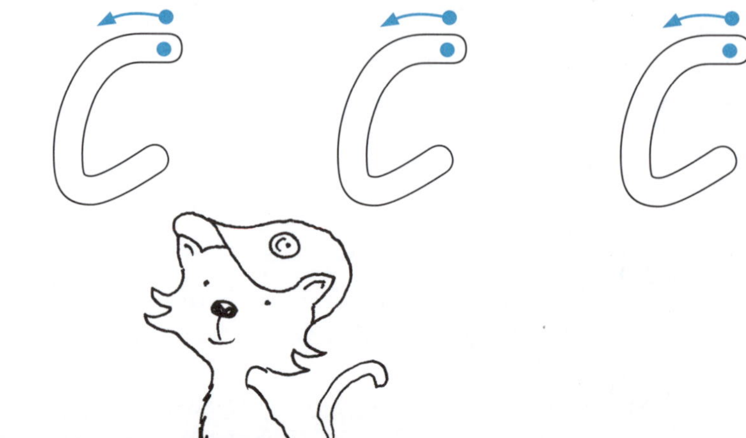

Handwriting: anticlockwise letter; body letter (c).
Vocabulary: cool, cow, cake, candle.
Phonic knowledge /k/: cat, can, cap, cup, cot, come.

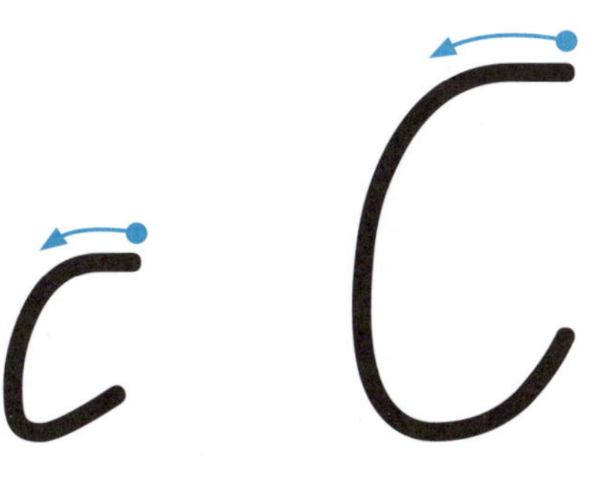

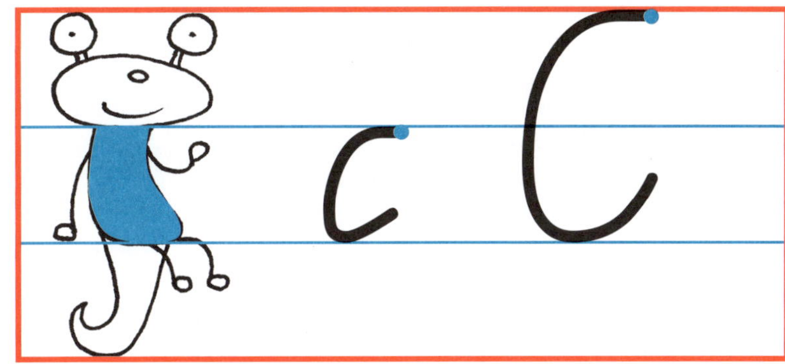

Track.

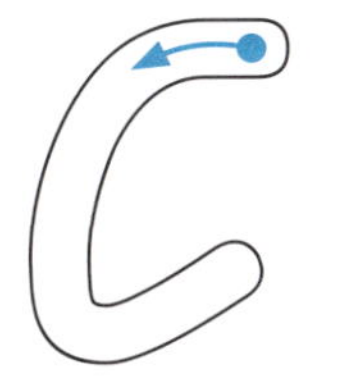 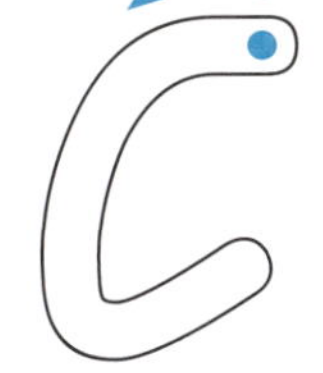     

Trace.

     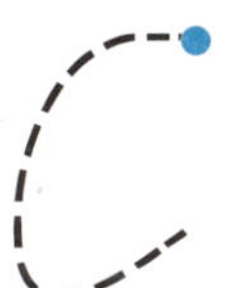 

Trace.

 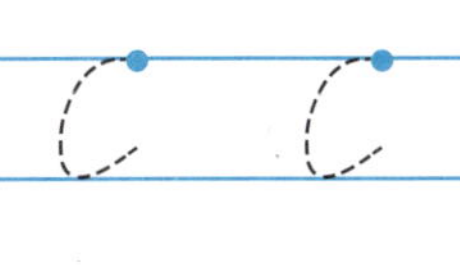 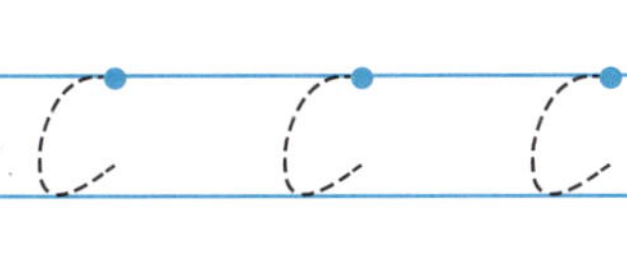 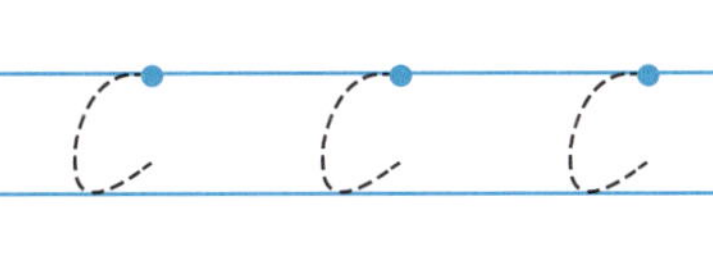 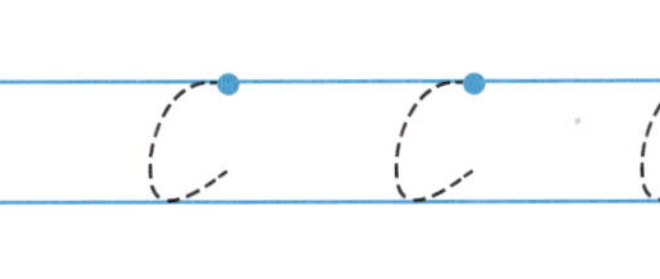 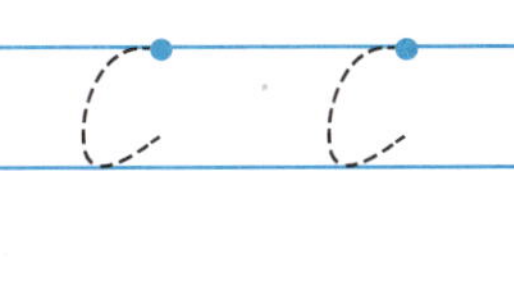 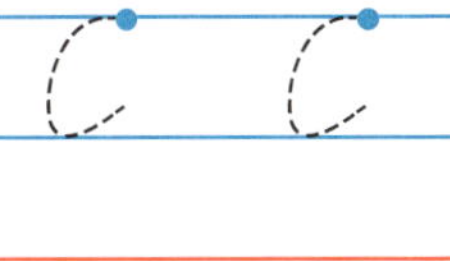 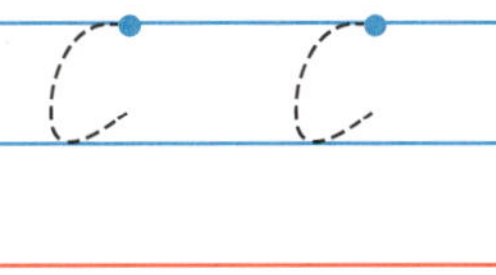

Write.

c

c

Patter

Go backwards then curve down, make a quick turn at the bottom. Keep your pencil on the page.

Phonic chant

frisky frog
f f f

Trace the pattern.

Trace the pattern. Keep your pencil on the page.

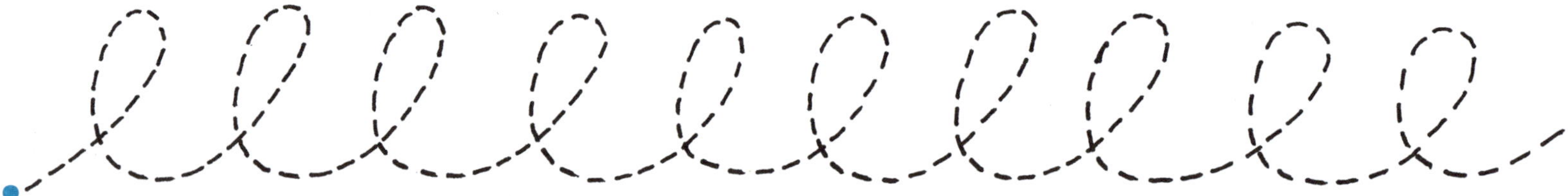

Find and write f.

f f f

Track.

f f f f f f f

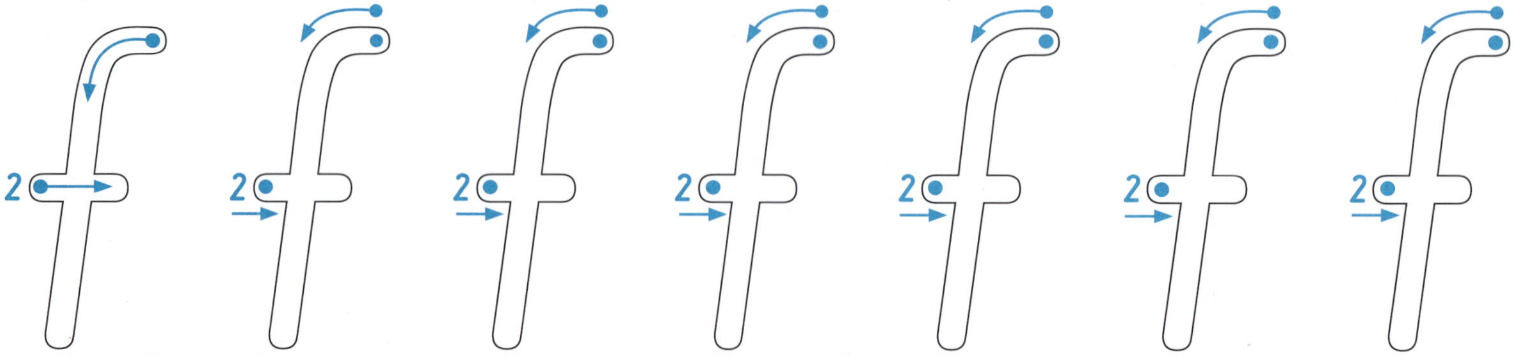

Handwriting: anticlockwise letter; head and body letter (ascender) (f).
Vocabulary: risky, frog, fish, flower.
Phonic knowledge /f/: fun, fin, fan , fit, fat, fog, if, puff, huff, cuff.

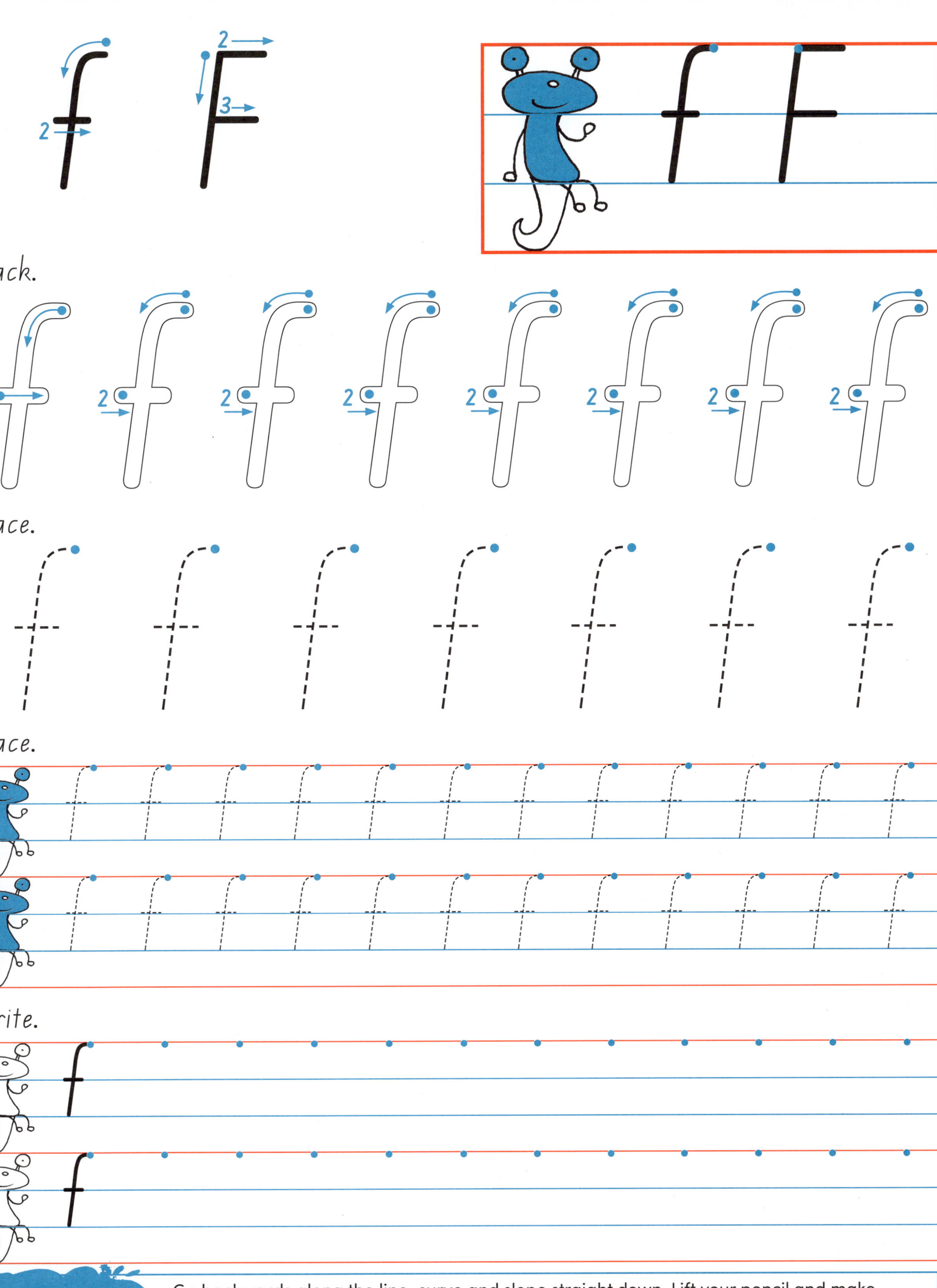

Patter

Go backwards along the line, curve and slope straight down. Lift your pencil and make a cross.

Phonic chant

giggly goanna

g g g

Trace the pattern.

Trace the pattern.

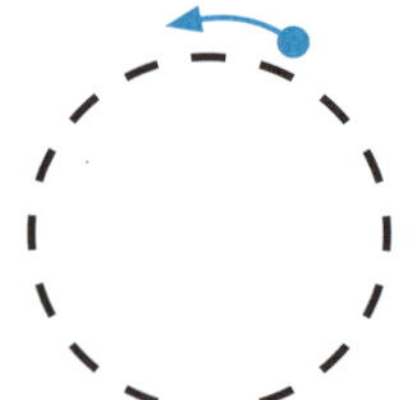  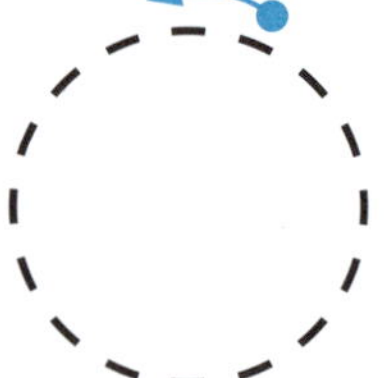 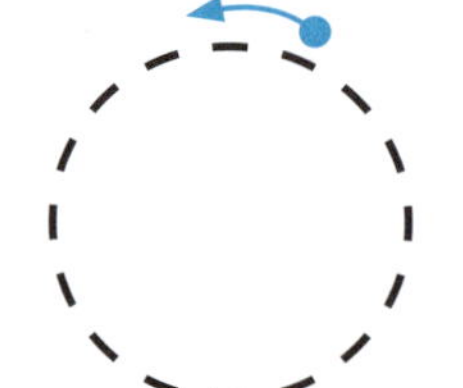 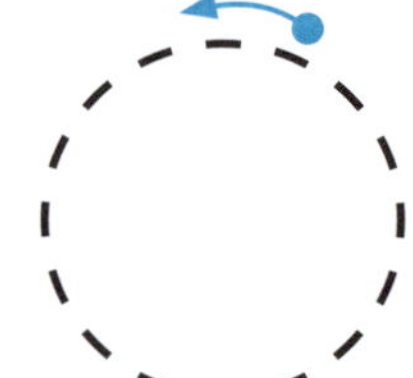 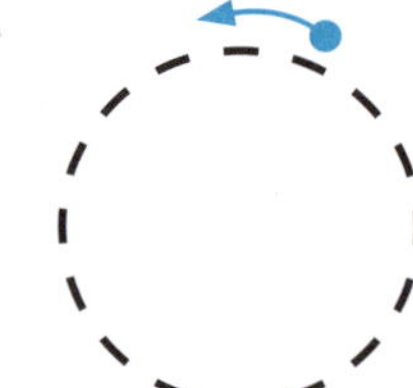

Trace the pattern.

Track.

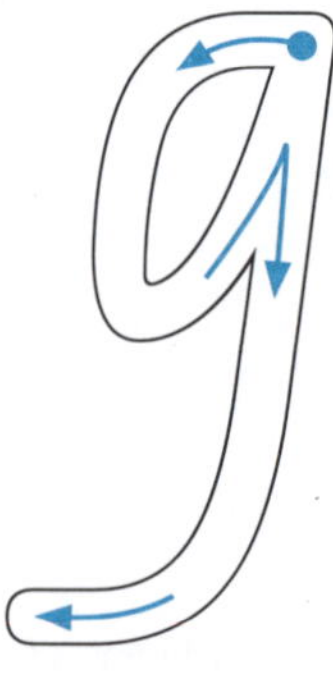  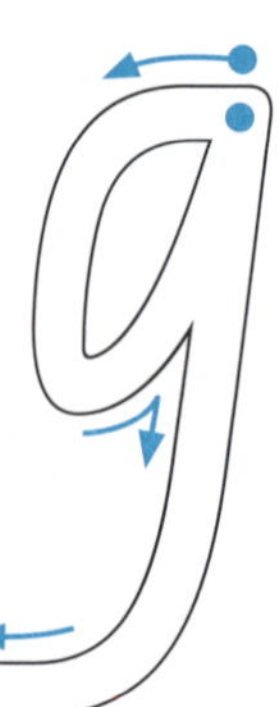 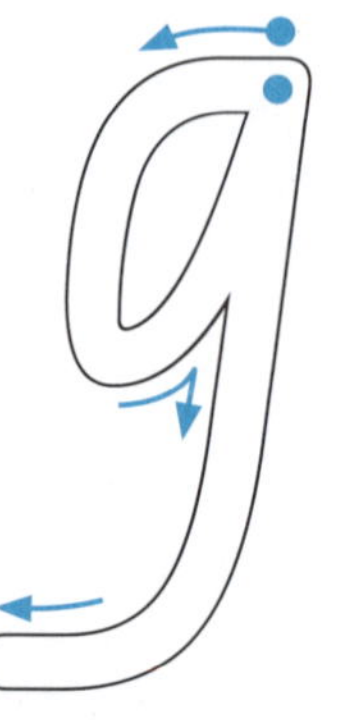 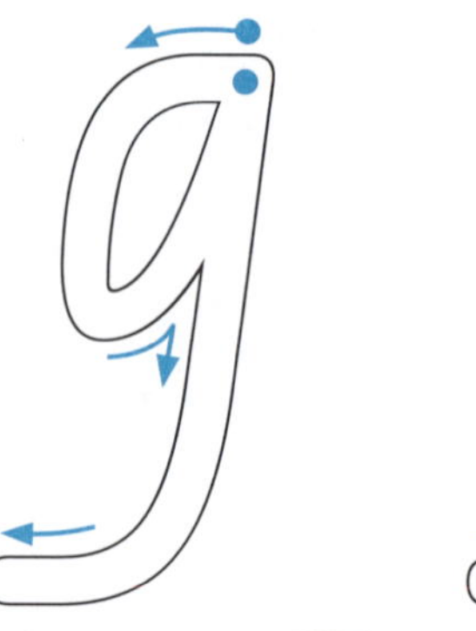 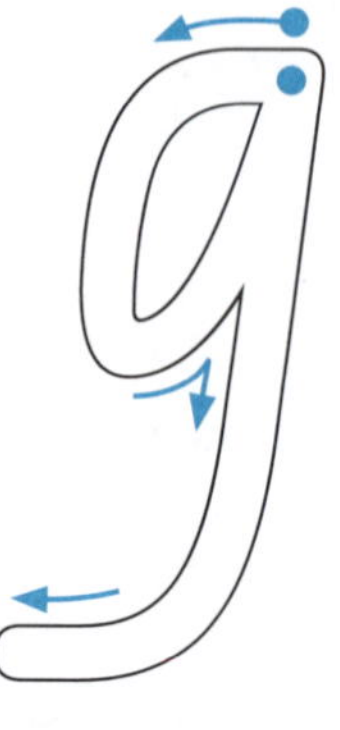

Handwriting: direction change letter; body and tail letter (descender) (g).
Vocabulary: giggly, goanna.
Phonic knowledge /g/: get, go, got, gas, pig, dig, dog, hog, tag, sag, egg.

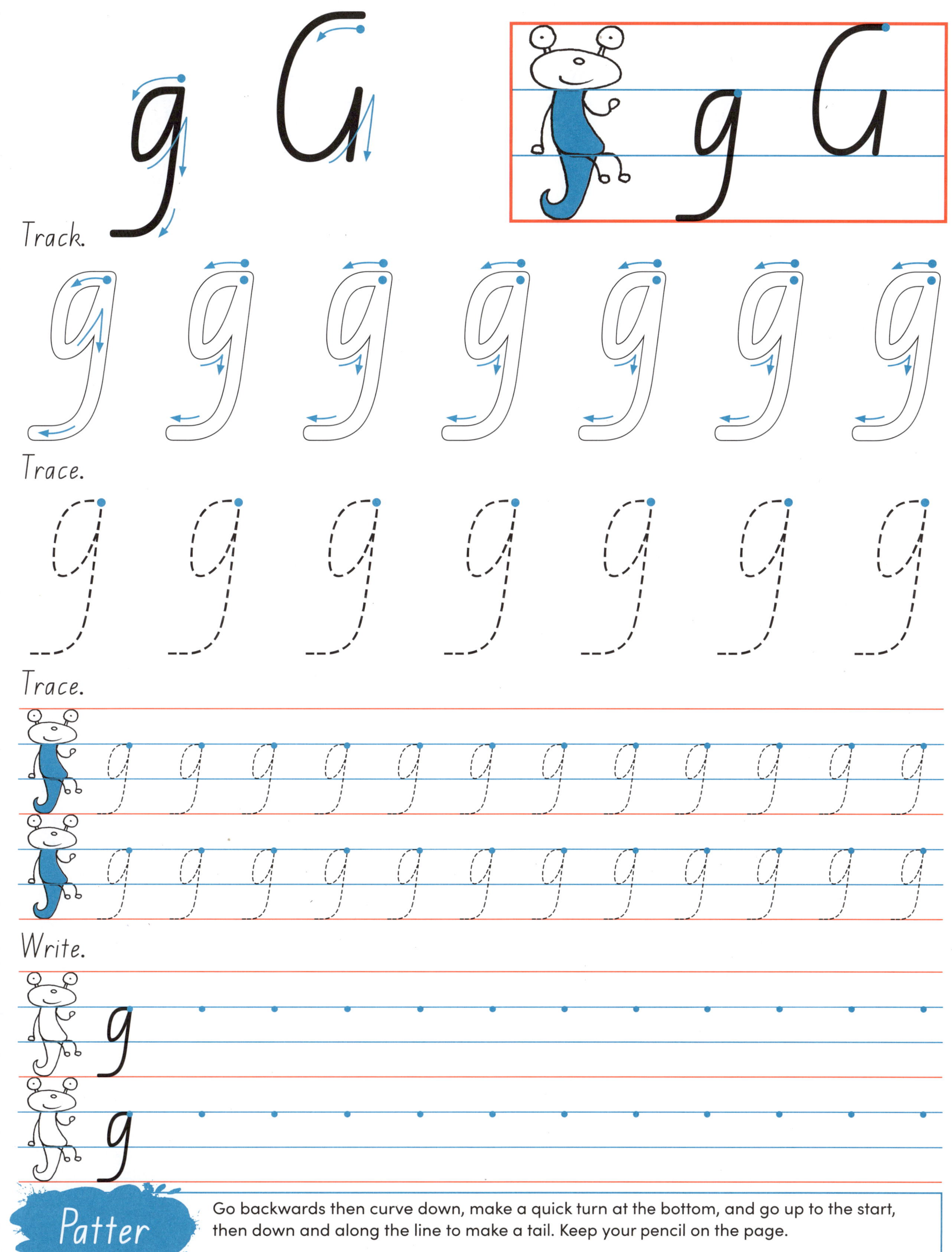

Go backwards then curve down, make a quick turn at the bottom, and go up to the start, then down and along the line to make a tail. Keep your pencil on the page.

Phonic chant

yellow yak

y y y

Trace the pattern.

Trace the pattern. Keep your pencil on the page.

Trace the pattern. Turn each pattern into a picture.

Track.

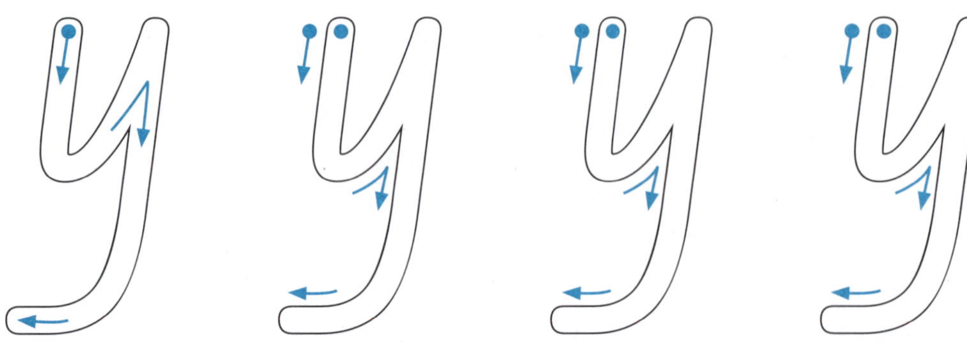

Handwriting: direction change letter; body and tail letter (descender) (y).
Vocabulary: yak, yellow, yo-yo.
Phonic knowledge /y/: yell, yes, yet, yap, yum.

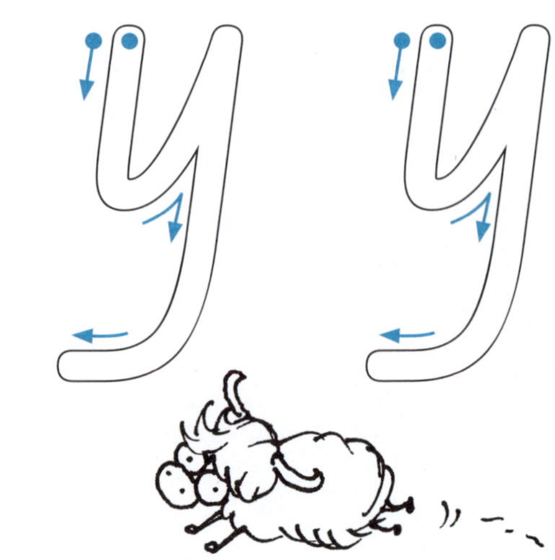

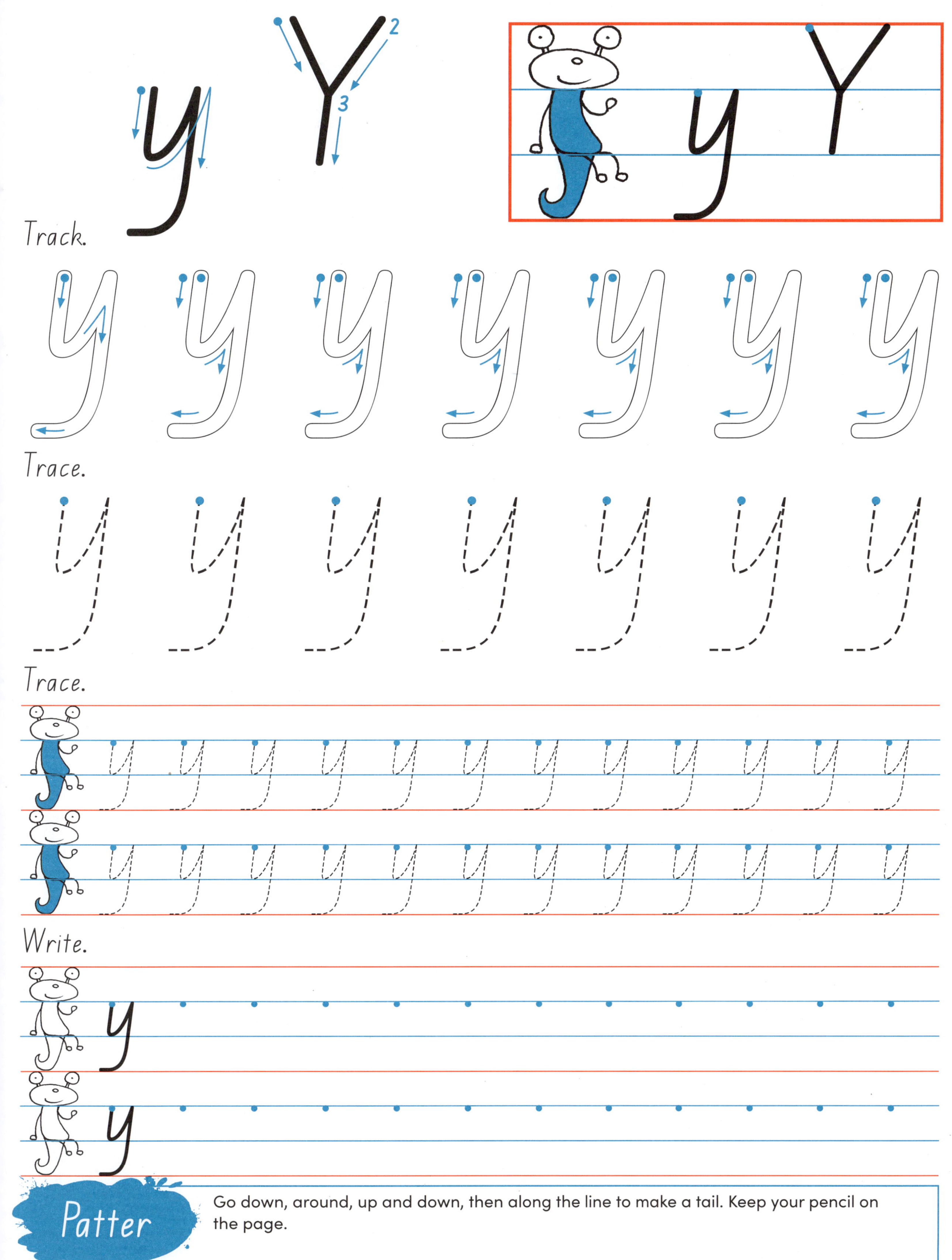

Patter

Go down, around, up and down, then along the line to make a tail. Keep your pencil on the page.

Phonic chant

slippery seal

s s s

Trace the pattern.

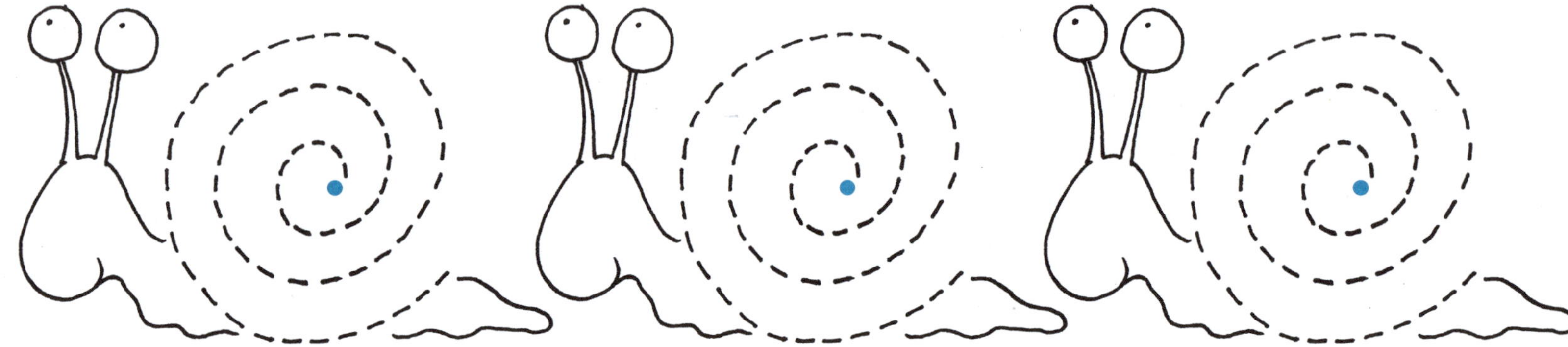

Trace the pattern. Turn the pattern into snakes.

Trace the pattern. Keep your pencil on the page.

Track.

Handwriting: direction change letter; body letter (s).
Vocabulary: snake, snail, seal, slippery, scissors, slip.
Phonic knowledge /s/: sat, sit, sip, so, six, sun.

Patter

Go backwards then change direction across the middle, then change direction and finish along the line. Keep your pencil on the page.

one ostrich 1
1
two tigers 2
2
Track.
Trace.
Write.
Trace the pattern.
Draw 1 thing.
Track.
Trace.
Write.
Trace the pattern.
Draw 2 things.

three thrushes 3
3
Track.
Trace.
Write.
Trace the pattern.
Draw 3 things.
four frogs 4
4
2
Track.
Trace.
Write.
Trace the pattern.
Draw 4 things.

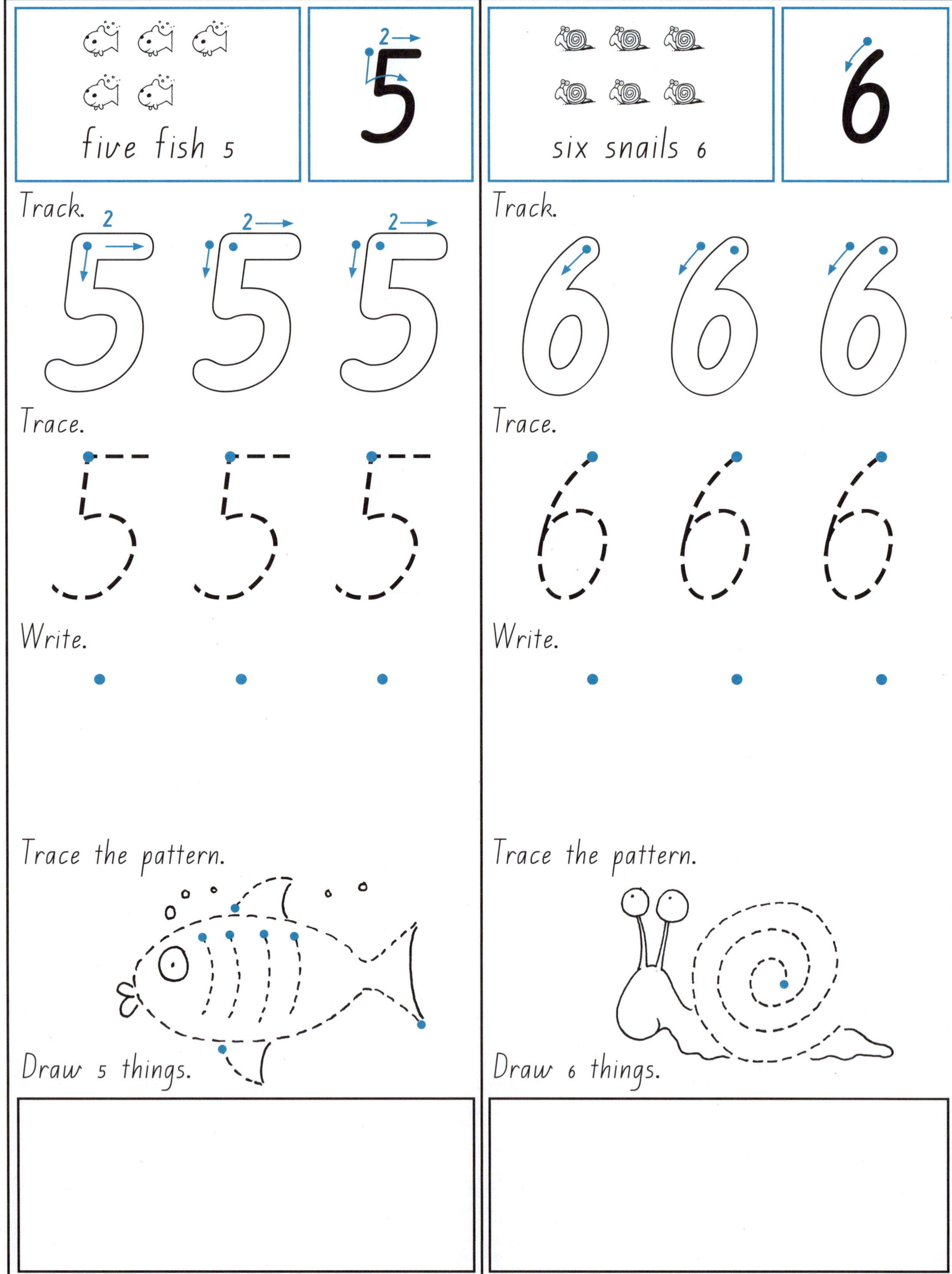
five fish 5
5
six snails 6
6
Track.
2
2
2
Track.
Trace.
Trace.
Write.
Write.
Trace the pattern.
Trace the pattern.
Draw 5 things.
Draw 6 things.

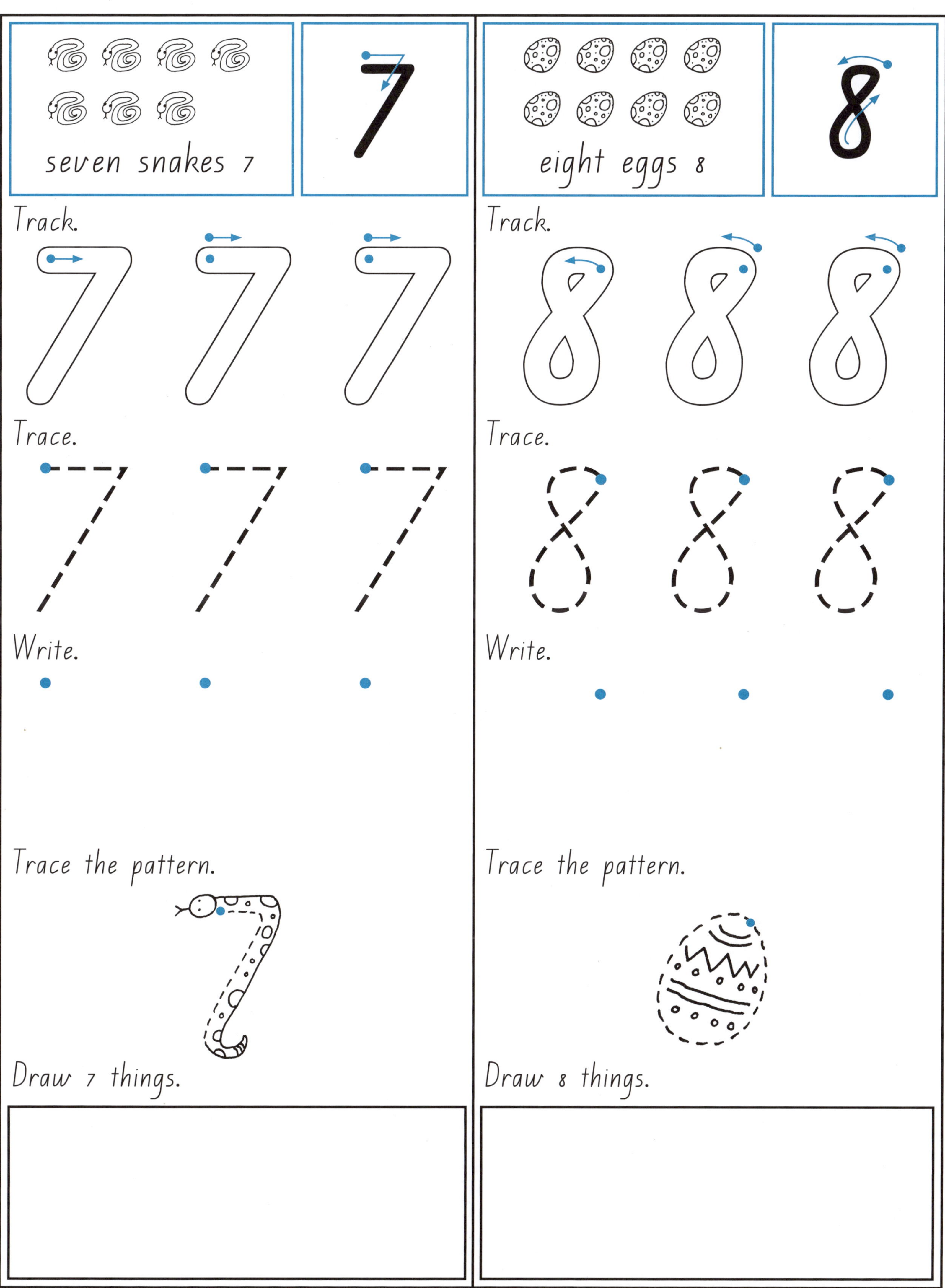
seven snakes 7
7
eight eggs 8
8
Track.
Trace.
Write.
Trace the pattern.
Draw 7 things.
Track.
Trace.
Write.
Trace the pattern.
Draw 8 things.

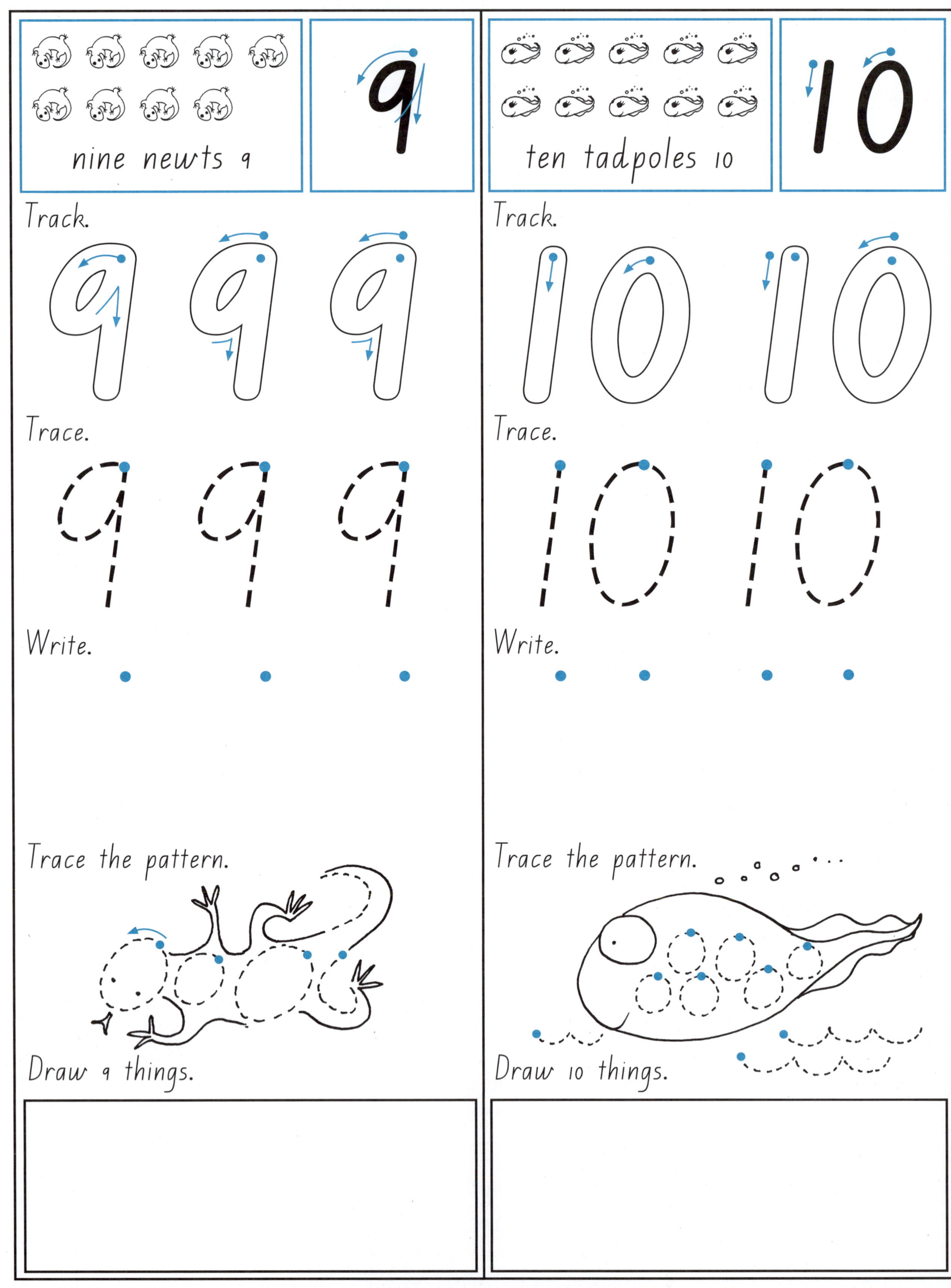
nine newts 9
9
ten tadpoles 10
10
Track.
Track.
Trace.
Trace.
Write.
Write.
Trace the pattern.
Trace the pattern.
Draw 9 things.
Draw 10 things.